IMPOSSIBLE NATION

THE LONGING FOR HOMELAND

IN CANADA AND QUEBEC

RAY CONLOGUE

THE MERCURY PRESS

The publisher gratefully acknowledges the financial assistance of the Canada Council
and the Ontario Arts Council.

Cover design by Gordon Robertson
Cover photograph by Peter Jones, copyright by Archive Photos, New York City, for
Reuters
Edited by Beverley Daurio
Composition and page design by TASK

Printed and bound in Canada by Metropole Litho
Printed on acid-free paper
First Edition
1 2 3 4 5 00 99 98 97 96

Canadian Cataloguing in Publication Data

Conlogue, Ray
Impossible nation : the longing for homeland in Canada and Quebec
Includes bibliographical references.
ISBN 1-55128-033-7
1. Canada - English-French relations.★ 2. Biculturalism - Canada.
3. Quebec (Province) - Civilization.   I. Title.
FC144.C648 1996   306.4'46'0971   C96-931717-4
F1027.C66 1996

Represented in Canada by the Literary Press Group
Distributed in Canada by General Distribution Services

The Mercury Press
137 Birmingham Street
Stratford, Ontario
Canada   N5A 2T1

À C.L., qui m'a fait comprendre.

To Charles Taylor, who has thought it through.

INTRODUCTION

On October 26, 1995, 100,000 Canadians gathered in Montreal's Dominion Square to persuade Quebec to stay in Canada.

Four days later, when their desperate gambit seemed to have carried the referendum vote to a narrow victory for Canada, these pilgrims became heroes. The deputy prime minister, tears in her eyes, thrilled to their patriotic gesture. Quebeckers, it was said, had been moved by a gesture of "love" from the anglophone majority.

But as the days and weeks went by, the truth gradually dawned: for the first time in history, more than half of Quebec's French-speaking population had voted to leave Canada once and for all. They had been forestalled only by the monolithic No vote of the province's English-speaking minority.

Anger set in. The media, never much inclined to explain the francophone perspective to English Canada, hardened into a bullying tone. French Canadians were characterized as racists who could not be trusted to preserve democracy in an independent Quebec. Some argued that Montreal would have to be seized and kept by Canada in order to protect the city's anglophones. Still others spoke ominously of the "illegality" of secession.

Virtually nobody seemed interested in understanding why Quebeckers felt as they did. Could this red-faced, stony-eyed Canadian people be the same one which had so recently declared its love for Quebec? Could they, indeed, be *my* people— the community in which I lived until coming to Montreal five years ago?

At the same time, living and working among francophones, it had become clear to me that an equally narrow and mistrustful view of English Canada is entrenched in Quebec. This is not to be confused with the attitude toward "les Anglais" within Quebec, where middle-class francophones are proud of their ability to speak English and often number anglophones among their friends. Their mental block is toward the rest of Canada, which they resist visiting and where their newspapers do not post correspondents. The attitude here is epitomized by a gentleman interviewed on the evening news who referred to Canada as "le pays en-dessous de nous" (the country underneath us). If secession has become a present danger, it is because of this profound *cultural* antipathy toward the entity called Canada— an antipathy which, it has now become clear, is reciprocated by English Canadians.

Throughout the country, university bookshelves groan under the weight of efforts made by historians, political writers and even philosophers to come to grips with our dilemma. Conspicuously absent, however, is cultural discussion. Little has been written in English about the poets and novelists who have articulated francophone nationalism for 150 years. Why is this, considering that almost everybody in Canada agrees that the problem is essentially cultural?

The massive descent of Canadians on Montreal last October is a metaphor for cultural deafness. The English speakers who went there thought they were demonstrating "love"; French-speaking Montrealers felt invaded by a callous throng with which they have nothing in common.

In 1876, Pierre Chauveau thought to compare the English and French in Canada to the famous double staircase of the Chateau de Chambord in Paris, whose characteristic is that two people can climb it simultaneously without seeing each other— except at the landings. "English and French, we climb by a double flight of stairs toward the destinies reserved for us on this continent, without knowing each other, without meeting each other, and without even seeing each other, except on the landing of politics."[1]

So it has remained. The relationship of English and French in Canada has withered to a sterile political argument, carried out at intervals on the landing. Our real lives, unglimpsed by the other, are carried out on the staircase.

This book was inspired by the crisis which occurred October 30, 1995, and will look at the idea that we have built a myth of national unity precisely because we have failed to build a bicultural country. And having failed, it is essential to our illusion of nationhood that we *not* know about Quebec, except for the occasional bit of folklore, filtered so as not to offend our sensibilities: Céline Dion singing in English on Canada Day; Roch Carrier's sentimental hockey sweater; Monique Mercure accepting a Governor General's award.

English Canada's particular tragedy has been to believe that it is partly French, even though the French themselves have not agreed to this and we ourselves have done little to give it substance. In order to sustain this invented identity, we forget our history and stifle our ears.

It is chastening to realize that five years ago, when I moved to Quebec, I saw nothing exceptional in the common lament: *How can Quebec complain when we have given it so much?* It took a long time to understand that assuming that "we" are in a position to bestow, rather than asking the minority what it requires for its survival, is by itself nearly enough to destroy a country.

It was a difficult evolution, and not one I had intended. My motives for going to Montreal in 1991 were largely personal. There was unfinished business with the French language, which I had begun to learn during a stay in North Africa in the early 1970's. As a *Globe and Mail* arts reporter, I was also aware that Quebec produced far more of our cultural output than could be explained by its population. It was evident that much of this activity was inspired by something vaguely called "nationalism," but I was less interested in the cause than in the abundant and luxuriant result: Robert Lepage's theatre, Denys Arcand's films, Hubert Aquin's novels.

Not long after arriving in Montreal, I began to feel profoundly disoriented (or, as French would have it, dépaysé: "de-countryed"). The National Institute for Scientific Research turned out to be a provincial entity; the Bibliothèque Nationale on St. Denis was not Canada's national library: it was Quebec's. And of course the provincial legislature was the Assemblée nationale.

In English Canada, history is dead and pinned to a board. In Quebec, it is alive. One summer night a random crowd gathered by the old city hall for a historic panorama enacted by giant puppets. When the Lord Durham puppet appeared with snot dripping from his nose and a cudgel hidden in his top hat, the crowd burst into lively hissing and booing. I stood dredging through half-remembered high school history. What exactly had he written in his famous Report to occasion this caricature? Evidently I was alone with my uncertainty.

As my French improved, so did my understanding of the experience of being a member of a linguistic minority in Canada. I began to sympathize with the observation of the bilingual Paul Tallard in Hugh MacLennan's novel *Two Solitudes*: "If you're completely at home in both languages... it makes it impossible to be enthusiastic about the prejudices of either of them." He adds: "... and that can be uncomfortable sometimes."[2]

I entered the "uncomfortable" phase. Watching Radio-Canada on TV, I became aware of the terrible French spoken by English-Canadian politicians. How, with the best language training money can buy, could they have learned so little? And why did they speak French with such displeasure, such joylessness? There were rare exceptions, such as Sheila Copps, who could use an expression like "c'est de la folie furieuse" with all the flair of a shopkeeper on Laurier Avenue. But her pleasure in the language— like so much else in her comportment— marked her as an eccentric English Canadian.

Dealing with anglo-Quebeckers was a delicate matter. Some of the anti-French bigotry of the past has disappeared, but the older generation— which is still setting the terms of political debate, and whose voice carries across Canada— has not lost the imperious mind-set of an earlier day. Television news announcers pointedly anglicize French names ("Today, Jack Pair-ee-zo met with Loosien Boo-shard..."). A reader of the Montreal *Gazette*, deafened by the daily anti-separatist perorations on the editorial page, combs the rest of the paper for the tiniest references to the city's vibrant French cultural life.

The younger anglo generation is more sympathetic. Among them, it is de rigueur to have at least some command of French. But they have inherited a tradition of disdain for francophones which goes back two centuries, and it emerges in their outright rejection of any thought of living in an independent French state.

Quebec's anglophones are at least aware that history is still alive and shaping their destiny. In this they are far ahead of English Canadians outside Quebec. Quebeckers who have visited or lived in Toronto or Vancouver are shocked by the empty clichés and the historical vacuum which they encounter there. Elsewhere in Canada, Quebec is represented as little more than an abstraction which occasionally becomes an annoyance.

It is strange that we have not made more progress. Thirty years ago there was general agreement not only to repair the historical injustices done to French speakers, but also to seek a general opening of the two cultures toward each other. We have largely accomplished the former, but the latter remains elusive. Why is this so?

Perhaps it is because the repairing of injustice can be done with the familiar toolkit of politics and economics. An Official Languages Act here, a grudging acceptance of a Bill 101 there, a little devolution of taxing powers, a clutch of bilingual bureaucrats, and voilà!

But all this is accomplished on the landing of the Chateau de Chambord's famous staircase. The activity in the stairwell— which is to say, daily life— is the realm of culture. And here, I believe, we are as we always have been.

Thirty years ago, while criss-crossing the country on behalf of the Royal Commission on Bilingualism and Biculturalism, André Laurendeau wrote in his diary that he was astonished by the "incuriosity" of the English-speaking population. People seemed "profoundly unconscious of the acuity of the problems" and unaware "of certain elements essential to Canadian reality."[3]

It troubled Laurendeau that people could not, or would not, see the difference between local provincial ethnic groups, such as the Mennonites or the Ukrainians, and the "organized society" of Quebec. He was dismayed at the general assumption that the French should be prepared to lose their language like any other "immigrant" group.

Like most francophone intellectuals, Laurendeau felt that people like himself— academics, newspaper editors— had a special responsibility to inform society and to defuse tensions. When university professors told him that they found it "very difficult" to learn to read French, much less speak it, his dismay became anger:

> Here there is a simple intellectual laziness, doubtless North American, and it prevents hundreds of university teachers from communicating directly with French Canada through journals, magazines and books. [This is a grave error] in a country where a third of the population speaks French."[4]

Thirty years later, less than a quarter of the Canadian population speaks French. Our élites remain innocent of the language. None of the senior anglophone officers in the armed forces can speak French, though required by law to do so. And academics, judging by the experience of a sociologist friend from the Université de Montréal, have not changed either. "Last year two of my colleagues gave a paper in French at their association's meeting in Vancouver," she recounts. "Nobody came. That is to say, nobody. Not one person."

These are the small things that wear out the souls of French Canadians. They don't like being invisible in their own country. Would you?

Biculturalism has failed in Canada, as it has failed elsewhere in the world. Different languages create an experiential gap which is difficult to cross. Even when Quebec writers are translated, the style of French rhetoric is off-putting to English readers. The few Quebec journalists who are heard in English Canada have mastered our style; that is to say, they have buried their own. Back in 1866, the translator of the first English version of François-Xavier Garneau's great history of Quebec warned his readers that he had been forced into "retrenchments of its exuberances... to meet the reasonable expectations of anglo-Canadian readers... Had the translator not taken some friendly freedoms with the text... the volumes would not be readable."[5]

And yet, goes the common belief, Canadians have made a good, true, honest attempt at biculturalism. We are an idealistic people. If anybody could have made this work, surely it is us?

Perhaps not. Individuals are often reproached for idealism because it prevents them from looking at practical solutions. The same is true of societies. When it comes to Quebec, English Canada prefers to solve imaginary problems rather than real ones. Idealists are especially vulnerable to sentimentality.

André Laurendeau felt that anti-intellectualism was a North-American phenomenon. So is idealism, whose language is that of sentiment. A critic recently pointed out that Huckleberry Finn, for all that he *felt* terrible about Jim's slavery, was not in fact prepared to do much about it. This becomes the template of the American way of dealing with social problems. One *feels* badly about them— and that's enough.

Canadians of good conscience certainly feel badly about Quebec. Unfortunately, they also feel that that's enough. This is the only way I can make sense of what Intergovernmental Affairs Minister Stéphane

Dion has called the "irrational" refusal of Canadians to respond to the near break-up of our country last October. People are sure that they have done enough, when in fact they have only felt enough. Hence the T-shirts worn by the demonstrators in Montreal last October: "Quebec, we love you." They didn't translate the slogans into French, they said, because... they forgot.

Emblematic of the power of forgetfulness is the hall of Canadian history in the majestic Museum of Civilization in Ottawa. Moving through the dioramas, one notices that somewhere in the middle of the eighteenth century the soldiers' uniforms cease being the blue of France and become the red of England. There is no explanation for this. The determining event of Canada's history, the Conquest of Quebec by the British in 1760, has been omitted.

The exhibit is (in an entirely unintended way) deeply honest. It illustrates an act of forgetting which Canadians carry out each day in a hundred ways in order to continue functioning as a nation.

It illustrates what happens when, on a popular level, we learn a few expressions in French and visit Quebec. We find it very charming, and vow that we will one day learn French "properly." Life is busy, and we don't get around to it, but our "intentions" were good; and that takes the place of the unperformed act.

Our best-loved writers, our Hugh MacLennans and Mordecai Richlers, live their lives on the interface of the two peoples without learning French. Other writers learn the language and live among those who speak it, but these argonauts are less popular: their work is "difficult," their characters "too subtle," their dilemmas too slippery and frustrating and... depressing.

Our public television network dutifully dubs and broadcasts Quebec's films and popular TV shows. Almost nobody watches them. In our own film and television, Quebeckers are almost completely absent.

Intellectuals who read French set about the Sisyphean task of pretending that French and English literatures in this country are two branches of a "national" literature. Even Northrop Frye convinced himself that Quebec poetry was a shrivelled thing because it seemed uninterested in the whole of Canada. If he had recognized that Quebec's writers were already describing *their* country, he would have had to confront the problem we can no longer escape.

And so the story unfolds, a diorama of national forgetting in a museum where we inter ourselves.

It is small comfort that we are not alone in this dilemma. No modern democracy has successfully functioned with two or more major language groups. Those that have come closest, Belgium and Switzerland, either separated the communities or are on the point of doing so. We may also be forced down this road, if we wish for any sort of entity called "Canada" to continue to exist.

But in Canada our problem is not only that we have two language groups. It is that the two groups have been pulled apart by historical currents that run much deeper than a difference of language. This has given rise to entirely different ideas of national "identity" in English and French Canada.

Quebec is a traditional society which took root before the ideas of the Enlightenment swept through Europe. English Canada, on the other hand, was founded much later by people who were marked by the doctrine of individualism and mistrustful of collective identity.

At the time of Confederation, it was recognized that the new country needed a collective identity. The efforts to spark such a thing were inhibited and self-conscious, but bore tentative fruit in the form of an early literary and artistic flowering.

By the beginning of this century, however, the competing force of American individualism had begun to pull English Canada's nascent nationalism to pieces. After World War II institutions such as the Canada Council were put in place to shore it up. Unfortunately, part of this process involved appropriating Quebec's Frenchness as part of Canada's new self-conscious identity-making: from that moment, English Canada closed its eyes to the fact that a separate, older, and much more firmly rooted cultural nationalism had already evolved in Quebec.

Quebec's struggle for cultural survival has depended on keeping the older collectivist idea alive, and it continues to do so. Today, this occasions much intolerance and misunderstanding on the part of English Canadians who find it "ethnic" or even "racist." What is truest about it, however, is that it saved Quebec's language and culture, and it will continue to be a force so long as Quebec feels that it is not "recognized" by English Canada.

A central preoccupation of this essay is the problem of "recognition" of minorities within national polities. This is a larger problem than the question of whether or not anglophones care to learn French. It has to do with the seeming inability of consituted nations to recognize the essential reality of "peoples" who exist within other nations and have not acceded to their own nation states.

The problem takes on a particular twist in Canada, where the English-speaking majority (it is generally agreed) has failed to develop a cultural identity commensurate with the possession of a nation state. At the same time, the French-speaking minority seems to have accomplished a cultural identity— but without obtaining a political state.

On a global scale, the issue of collective "recognition" is a reaction against the liberal individualism that has dominated Western countries since late in the last century. In this sense, Quebec's nationalism is not a relic, but rather the survival of a powerful idea which is once again on the rise.

Part of our difficulty in giving "recognition" to Quebec is that, superficially, it has come to resemble the rest of North America. Quebeckers' music is American in style, they are fiercely efficient consumers, holidayers in Florida, followers of fashion from The Gap and Benetton. It is hard today to fill a hall for the patriotic ruralistic warbling of Gilles Vigneault. Their continued insistence on their "distinct" society is sometimes called, by unsympathetic observers, little more than the narcissism of minor differences.

But contemporary Quebec has kept the profound reflexes which it has inherited from the past, for reasons both conscious and unconscious. Contemporary Quebec art— film and theatre particularly— shows how artists still feel the grinding pressure of the English language, and how much effort they must devote to persuading both themselves and their public that it is worthwhile to continue the struggle to live in French.

On an unconscious level, the society still has reflexes of mutual support and affirmation which are virtually non-existent in English Canada. It is routine for a Quebec novelist like Réjean Ducharme to be compared with James Joyce, or a filmmaker like Gilles Carle to take his place in the pantheon with François Truffaut or Billy Wilder. In a meditation on poets who have written about the dawn, *Le Devoir* sees no incongruity in listing local writers with the giants of French art and literature. "Rimbaud, Baudelaire, Monet, Debussy, our Felix Leclerc with *Barefoot in the Dawn*, Vigneault in *The Bows of Ships...*" Quebeckers simply have no doubt that they are as good as anybody else. Given their small population, it is an assertion which is bound to be frequently exaggerated and even absurd; but who can doubt that it is profoundly healthy for a people who wish to take their place as a nation in the world?

The result is the creation of a "place." Television talk shows scroll a pantheon of local stars in front of a vast public. A short-story contest's sole prize is that the winner's work will be read aloud by novelist Yves Beauchemin. Leaders— political, religious, artistic— are regularly thrown up to incarnate Quebec's values; when they die, their funerals are public events.

English Canadians look upon this with a mixture of envy and dismay— contradictory feelings which help explain why our own nationalism has failed to take flight. We have a strong attachment to our regional landscapes, and we have created a flourishing literature. But we have not bonded with our country as a whole.

Making a virtue of necessity, many Canadians argue that nationalism as such is a rusted-out and irrelevant idea. But there is a very good argument that liberal individualism, which leaves us free to create only private meaning in our lives, has done all that it can. From where will we acquire the necessary sense of belonging to something larger than ourselves?

It is clear from our recent political behaviour that we are not finding this sense of belonging by endlessly juggling constitutional formulas or wearing other people's costumes in the sad pantomime of multiculturalism.

Canada needs to learn from Quebec; particularly if Canada must, one day soon, make its way without Quebec.

CHAPTER ONE

When our narrow rooms, our short lives, our soon ended passions and
emotions put us out of conceit with sooty and finite reality, here at last
is a universe where all is large and intense enough to almost satisfy the
emotions of man. — W.B. Yeats on nationalism

It is rare to find a nationalist who can recognize a nationalist of another
and hostile nation. — D.W. Brogan

When just a shade under half of Quebec's population voted to secede
from Canada in October, 1995, the shock to English Canadians everywhere was visceral. In the political realm, secession is the only gesture
which can deliver an emotional blow similar to that of a family death or
marital break-up. This near-secession was, millions of people could not
help feeling, a rejection of *them*.

Human nature provides a cushioning reflex to deflect such assaults,
and defensiveness was not long in manifesting itself. The tabloid press
across Canada emitted a howl of rage, characterizing those who would
leave Canada as bigots, ethnic cleansers, tribalists, a "band of fanatics."
The elected premier of Quebec was associated with the builders of gas
chambers, and the *Financial Post* declared that Jacques Parizeau was bent
on purifying Quebec of its anglophones and its immigrants.

Quebec separatism has been maturing toward a final break with
Canada for the past 30 years, but Canadians have been unable to come
to grips with it. It is not hard to understand why. The qualities that make
our country so attractive to others and to ourselves— a century-and-a-half
of domestic peace, a comfortable standard of living, an idealized notion
of ourselves as a kind and gentle people— are the worst possible qualities
for dealing with a crisis of this kind. We have little experience of hard

decisions, and we have never learned to admit challenges to the status quo into public discourse. As André Laurendeau expressed it in 1964: "There is an astonishing absence of self-criticism throughout English-Canadian society."[1]

This lack of self-criticism and our well-known difficulty in defining a national identity are connected. We agree that we don't have a strong culture, that we don't respect our artists and writers, that the task of overcoming our philistinism about our own achievements always seems to lie before us.

Asked to explain *why* this is so, however, we fall silent. Or we argue that there is no reason why it should be so, because we live in quite a wonderful country.

And we muddle on. We are that strangely distracted people who cannot quite listen to our singers, remember our history, or find our voice when a beloved leader dies. We are the land, as Alice Munro puts it, where the confident are silenced with the imperious question, "Who do you think you are?" One of the writers in whom we take the most pride, Robertson Davies, wrote in *Murther and Walking Spirits*: "You don't love Canada; you are part of Canada, and that's that."[2]

We have the impression that this is a solvable problem, one for which we will eventually find the right constitutional wording, the right way of talking to Quebec, the correct infusion of self-esteem. But what if it is not a solvable problem? If that is the case, then English Canadians do not merely happen to avoid it: we are *obliged* to do so.

I think that is the case, because the root problem has to do with irreconcilable ideas of nationalism. Quebeckers consider themselves to be a "people," an idea which comes from a tradition usually called romantic or "cultural" nationalism. English Canada, on the other hand, believes itself to be an instance of "civic" nationalism, an idea which has different historic roots.

To make matters worse, English Canadians have, at the same time, a nostalgia for cultural nationalism, a desire to be a "people" distinct from others— especially Americans. To complete the confusion, we have created a myth of national unity which maintains that Quebec is part of whatever we decide Canada to be; that is, that Quebec's "peopleness" must somehow seamlessly meld with our own to create a new "people." But, as we shall see, historically such a fusion of different cultural nationalisms is impossible; indeed, it is a kind of sin against nature— especially when the peoples in question speak different languages.

One begins to see why we refrain from self-criticism.

Most modern nation states, with the possible exception of Great Britain (which managed it a little earlier), came into existence after the American and French revolutions. These were, like Canada, democratic states which offered citizens equal rights and an equal sense of membership.

But most of these new countries, which by the late nineteenth century included Germany, Italy, Greece and many of the other familiar European states, also came with a de facto ethnic identity. That is, they shared elements of a common language, literature and history. Their citizens were united by more than individual rights; they also had a collective cultural heritage which conferred on them a sense of pride and belonging.

Since the Enlightenment began shortly after 1700, the dominant idea in western societies has been that of individualism and universal human rights. Nationalism, however, comes from a competing historic idea based on the irreducible need of human beings to belong to a community. The new states resolved this uncomfortable contradiction by claiming that their democracies had evolved something called "civic" nationalism, which distinguished them from unhappy states having "ethnic" nationalism, where those not part of the dominant group had fewer rights, or none at all.

This overstated, even Manichean distinction is still with us. An example occurs in Michael Ignatieff's recent book about nationalism, *Blood and Belonging*. "Civic nationalism," he writes, "maintains that the nation should be composed of all those— regardless of race, colour, creed, gender, language, or ethnicity— who subscribe to the nation's political creed."[3]

According to this notion, one of the freedoms of people living in a democracy is freedom of language. But in actual fact, almost all of the modern nation states— with the painful and particular exception of Canada— use a single language.

In some of these countries, uniformity of language is a happy coincidence, a historical residue. But others, particularly Great Britain, France and the United States, had to fall back on "the introduction of linguistic uniformity"[4] in order to deal with groups that didn't speak the dominant language. In France, languages like Breton and Occitan, which had happily perked along for centuries, were eliminated by state policy in less than 100 years. In the United States, colonies that had been founded by non-English peoples— the Dutch in New York, the Germans in Pennsylvania— saw their large populations assimilated less than 50 years after the revolution. The francophones of Louisiana took longer. It was necessary until 20 years ago to beat children who persisted in speaking French in school, but now the language is effectively extinct south of the 49th parallel.

Why? The usual reason given is practical: that the other "civic" freedoms depend on easy communication among citizens, for which a common language is essential.

But it remains an uncomfortable fact that a common language is also one of the profound requirements of "ethnic" nationalism. Here the reason given is not practical, but has to do with meaningfulness and belonging, with the sharing of a common culture and outlook on the world.

At the time of Confederation, in 1867, all the countries of the western world were wrestling with this dilemma.

The idea of formal individual rights created a profound excitement which can still be sensed by a reading of the American Constitution. It was the motivating principle of the French and American revolutions, and it created what has been called "the first wave of modern nations."[5]

But it wasn't long before a reaction set in. Humanist thinkers were repelled by the idea which emerged with Locke and Hume that nature might be no more than a sort of large mechanical toy waiting to be exploited by atomized human beings with loyalty to no-one but themselves. Was there no meaning in nature, or in our relationship with it? they wondered.

Their reaction took the form of the Romantic movement, and its political expression was nationalism. Where the Enlightenment suggested that a nation was little more than a contract, nationalist thinkers claimed that humanity was divided into "natural" nations which had evolved in close relationship with the physical environment. Everything about such a community, from its customs to its shared history— but especially its language— was an expression of its organic relationship with the natural world. It had an inherent right to become a political nation.

This was the idea behind the "second wave" of nations, the popular uprisings which created the German, Italian and Greek states in the mid-nineteenth century.

In pre-Confederation Canada there was a lively competition between these ideas, with many people attracted to America's extreme expression of individual rights. But Canada was the home of two peoples speaking different languages. And the French, as a diminishing minority in North America, were concerned above all for their collective survival. In the late 1700's and early 1800's, the United States was threatening to annex the British colonies, and its evolving "linguistic uniformity" was already quite evident to the French Canadians. "The French Canadians had entered Confederation not to protect the rights of the individual," writes philosopher George Grant, "but the rights of a nation."[6]

And therein lay the dilemma. If Canada itself was to be a nation, how could there be another nation seeking protection within it?

Matters were complicated by the fact that Great Britain, that other "first wave" modern nation, had also had a wee problem with linguistic minorities— to wit, countries speaking Irish, Scots and Welsh respectively— which it had gobbled up. These languages were being systematically destroyed in the early nineteenth century, about the same time France was doing in its minority languages. My great-grandmother, who was a refugee from the Irish famine of the 1840's, was also a refugee from the forced anglicization of Ireland which had been underway since the 1820's. She still spoke Irish when she arrived in the Ottawa Valley, but was so traumatized by what she had seen— and the fact she was still living in a British possession— that she flatly refused to teach the language to her daughter, my grandmother.

Linguistic intolerance was ingrained in the English settlers who came to Canada. Between the Conquest of 1760 and Confederation in 1867, it was twice officially proclaimed (and once unofficially) that the French would be forcibly anglicized. These policies didn't last long— for the obvious reason that French Canadians at the time were not a minority in Canada, but rather a vast majority. Who exactly was going to force them?

The policies also failed for the less obvious reason that the French already thought of themselves as a "people." The ideas of romantic nationalism had reached Quebec by the 1820's, long before Confederation, and were enthusiastically expressed in an outburst of novels, poems, and popular histories. By 1837, the Canadiens were quite ready to create themselves as a "second wave" modern nation with a strong ethnic identity. They even tried to do it the romantic way, with muskets.

The uprising failed, but the will to create a nation simply went underground. Instead of seeking political independence, French Canadians (in the expression of Quebec sociologist Fernand Dumont) set out to build a "cultural nation." When their representatives sat down to negotiate the terms of Confederation, it was with the idea that Quebec would be the home of this cultural nation. In essence, the Canadiens proposed to erect a state on the principle of romantic nationalism *within* a larger state committed to civic nationalism. Canada implicitly accepted the deal, on condition that future western provinces be English-speaking.

Since, as we have seen, these two kinds of nationalism are not as distinct as their respective partisans pretend, there was a good deal of confusion from the beginning. Also, within English Canada itself there was an influential strain of romantic nationalism which showed up shortly after Confederation in the "Canada First" literary movement. To read some of this movement's poetry today, with its emphasis on the achievements of sturdy Anglo-Saxons defying the rigours of a northern land, is to be in no doubt at all about its ethnic provenance.

But there was this difference between English and French Canada: that while the English were divided between the cultural and civic models of nationalism, the French were very clear and committed to the former. For them, given the reality of their situation in North America, there was no other way.

English Canadians suffered, and continue to suffer, enormously from the pull between the two forms of nationalism. Perceiving early on that there could be nothing to distinguish our civic nationalism from that of the Americans, who speak the same language we do, we set out to build a structure of cultural nationalism that would distinguish our "nation" from their "nation."

The problem here was, which culture? In the early days, the answer was clearly British, since most English Canadians were Orange Protestants with a zealous attachment to the glories of the British Empire. It led to deathless poetry such as this from John Gay: "Hail our great Queen in her regalia: One foot in Canada, the other in Australia."

Although we like to think fondly of him today, Stephen Leacock illustrates why this imperial strain was doomed. In a perfectly serious utterance, he advanced the view that the Ukrainian farmers flooding west at the turn of the century would one day feel a tug in their hearts and tears in their eyes at the mention of Nelson's exploits at Trafalgar.

This did not come to pass. Romantic nationalists recognize that history cannot move the hearts of a people unless it is *shared* history. The necessity to populate the empty west meant that more and more English-speaking Canadians would not have an ancestral connection to England.

Thoughtful Canadians were aware as early as the first decade of this century that Canada's Britishness was being replaced with Americanness. The United States is an enormous machine for atomizing communities, and in 1900 it was just getting into high gear. Young English Canadians evidenced very little interest in writing national epics, and much more in becoming consumers. They were rapidly losing interest in the exploits of their ancestors and the glories of their religion. The country could only survive if a truly Canadian identity were erected in place of the decaying British one.

In following this line of thought, policy makers implicitly admitted a particular usefulness of nationalism: that when a country is threatened with absorption by a powerful neighbour, nothing but culture will do to create the collective will necessary to meet the threat. (This, of course, also applies to Quebec, but it is part of the intellectual double bind of English–Canadian nationalism not to see this.)

For this reason, organizations like the the Canadian Broadcasting Corporation and the Canada Council were given mandates which, however diluted and sweetened, still bore the imprint of romantic nationalism. It can be seen in the hearty determination to help Canadians "tell their stories" to each other and to reflect the particular geography in which they live.

With the tide of rabid Britishness ebbing away, English Canada could have decided at this point to make common cause with the cultural nationalism that was already deeply rooted in Quebec. There could have been an acknowledgement that both peoples were trying to create organic and separate identities for themselves, in line with the principles laid down by the romantic philosophers. Our originality would have been to do this within a single political state.

But this was not to be. To begin with, a heritage of bigotry against French Canadians had begun at the time of the Conquest and has been zealously pursued ever since. Illegal laws were passed in New Brunswick, Ontario, Manitoba and Saskatchewan to suppress French schools. There was the idea, less frequently uttered aloud, but widespread, that Lord Durham had been right: Quebec's was a backward people, a doomed culture, a population that could only be saved by being anglicized. One did not hold out one's hand to offer an equal partnership to such people.

"We British Canadians possess a sense of racial superiority which seems to be innate in us, and which we do not acknowledge even to ourselves," wrote W. Eric Harris in 1927. "Deep-rooted in us is a feeling that the man who speaks a foreign language, who belongs to another race, must be inferior to ourselves, and we treat him, in spite of ourselves perhaps, with a mixture of a little pity and a small contempt. Whether we have openly shown to the French Canadian this sense of superiority, or have subtly inferred it, nevertheless he feels its existence, and this does not help the development of that co-operation which is essential to the national welfare."[7]

Religious passions ran so high in the 1920's that Harris felt he had to reassure his readers that he was a loyal Orangeman. He was a courageous writer, and a perceptive one. He had already noticed what Laurendeau would perceive nearly 40 years later: that absence of English-Canadian self-criticism, that refusal to "acknowledge even to ourselves."

Where did it come from? It may have served to mask a conflict deep within British Canadians. On the one hand, the rise of Orangeism after 1850 had given them a taste of ethnic passion. On the other hand, the older Puritan tradition, expressed in the ideas of John Locke, enjoined them to an extreme individualism, an almost pathological mistrust of collective belief and action. Locke had argued that we should "wrest control of our thinking and outlook away from passion or custom or authority, and assume responsibility for it ourselves."[8] These ideas also lay behind American expansionism, which helps to explain why many British Canadians, in spite of themselves, were fascinated with America.

None of this was good news for the French, who, with their attachment to Catholicism and community, seemed to deserve the "little pity and a small contempt" which generations of English-Canadian children lapped up with their morning cereal (unilingual boxes, please) and school history books.

At the same time, English Canadians had a residual affection for the idea of cultural nationalism, for the idea of being a people rooted and secure in its homeland. When they weren't busy disliking the French, they were secretly envious of them. Again, W. Eric Harris:

> We do not give our French-Canadian brother the credit for being the able and cultured man he is. We ourselves become more American each day, and it is well for Canada that we have in Quebec a people who hold fast to the older, sounder traditions of life. The attractions of materialism do not take hold of them as they do of us. There, there remains a sense of the beautiful, a love of song and legend, an attachment to duty.[9]

Gradually, the idea took hold in English Canada that, however desirable a cultural identity might be, actually creating one was a rather disagreeable and *unsophisticated* business. Perhaps building a culture could somehow be delegated, or subcontracted, to these French Canadians, who seemed to have such an enthusiasm for it. "You could easily write a dozen adjectives beside the name of the Englishman and everyone would recognize him," wrote Bruce Hutchison in 1942. "The Canadian, however, leaving aside the distinctive and clear-cut people of Quebec, is still a blur."[10]

Hutchison saw hope in what he called an evolving Canadian character that would be a blend of English and French. Like many anglophones who thought this way, he was perfectly aware— but preferred not to see— that the two groups lived separately, rarely intermarried, and generally knew nothing about each other. Describing a visit to Quebec City, Hutchison unwittingly describes this split mind-set: "Always as I walk these quiet streets I feel that behind the walls is a life, strange, exotic, rich, that I shall never see or know. Probably there are only ordinary people on the other side of these shutters... but I will never believe it."[11]

Because this notion that the folkloric French could help us create a cultural identity was little more than wishful thinking, English Canadians continued to rely on the decaying Britishness of Canada to anchor themselves. My own childhood memories go back just far enough to recollect the last gasp of the old Orange ethnicity. In the 1950's, children in my suburban Toronto neighbourhood— with names like Gale, Haddow, Bentley— still grouped themselves by religion, hurling the epithets "Catholic" and "Protestant" at each other. For the longest time I thought the latter word was spelled Proddisin, and I had not the least clue what it meant apart from its association with a few elderly men on knackered-out white horses who clopped through downtown Toronto each summer in a sad little parade.

A well-meaning élite of the Vincent Massey variety tried to foster a new sense of identity strictly rooted in Canada, but this didn't work too well. It did produce a certain flowering, of which the paintings of the Group of Seven were the most striking example. But the language of romantic nationalism which went with it already seemed archaic and even embarrassing in anglophone North America. It is "only through the deep and vital experience of its total environment that a people identifies itself with its land," wrote Lawren Harris in 1948. "We [the Group of Seven] were convinced that no virile people could remain subservient to and dependent upon the creations in art of other peoples... To us there was also the strange brooding sense of another nature fostering a new race and a new age."[12]

By the 1960's, when I was a student, there erupted among the artistic and intellectual élite a much more aggressive cultural nationalism directed against American penetration of our country, part of an international revulsion against the vacuity and materialism of the world which had been left to us by the Enlightenment. Indeed, "flower power" can be seen as a resurgence of the romantic idea, of the search for meaning. In many places it encouraged bonding with one's local land and history, nowhere more so than in Canada, where it helped foster the first great generation of Canadian novelists— Margaret Laurence, Michael Ondaatje, Margaret Atwood.

Unfortunately, the underlying nationalism of most English Canadians had by then become so diffuse and "civic" that the new movement did not last long or accomplish much. Today Canadian movies can still not be seen in Canadian theatres, and our legitimate theatre, founded with much fanfare in the sixties, has collapsed before a tidal wave of international mega-musical drivel. When the Mulroney conservatives, with their continentalist bent, began, in the mid-eighties, to dismantle the few modest policies that had been put in place to protect Canadian culture, "most of the country yawned."[13]

This development was foreseen by one of the great thinkers of the Canadian mid-century, George Grant. In 1966, in *Lament for a Nation*, Grant argued that Canada was finished as a state because none of its élites, especially the business élite, were committed to cultural nationalism. Therefore there could be no real opposition to the American model, which took its "thought from the eighteenth-century Enlightenment. [Its] rallying cry was 'freedom.' There was no place in their cry for the organic conservatism that predated the age of progress."[14]

Grant defined this conservatism as "the right of the community to restrain freedom in the name of the common good." Canada had once had such a conservatism, which generated a "common intention among its people" to resist absorption by the United States. It was behind the constitutional arrangements of 1791 and those of Confederation. "Both [French and English] peoples recognized that they could only be preserved outside the United States of America" since America was a country which "has always demanded that all autonomous communities be swallowed up into the common culture"[15] as the price of individual rights.

Grant wished that the different conservatisms of the two founding peoples "could have become a conscious bond" so that "this nation might have preserved itself."[16] But alas, the nationalist tradition inherited from Britain was not "philosophically explicit."[17]

French Canada, on the other hand, was strongly rooted. He believed that it would resist absorption much longer than English Canada, but that the forces arrayed against organic human communities in the twentieth century were ultimately irresistable. Reaching for the elegiac tone, he pronounced "French-Canadian nationalism... a last-ditch stand. The French on this continent will at least disappear from history with more than the smirks and whimpers of their English-speaking compatriots— with their flags flying and, indeed, with some guns blazing."[18]

As Grant wrote those words, the precursor groups of the Parti Québécois were already being founded in Montreal. Although few of the political architects of the Quiet Revolution sought independence for Quebec, they had unleashed a great upwelling of cultural nationalism which had both the good and bad qualities of such a movement. It exaggerated the injustices suffered by Quebeckers, and made a gentle singer like Félix Leclerc write songs about "the anger that slips between a man's skin and his soul." But it also tapped into a genuine current of romantic nationalism which had first bubbled up 150 years earlier, and which— unnoticed by a patronizing and self-preoccupied English Canada— has flowed uninterrupted ever since.

When it first became apparent that Quebec might actually strike out for independence, the attitude of English Canada changed overnight. Gone was the fond old folkloric prose, wherein a hollow-cheeked secessionist could be dismissed as a "mountebank" by Bruce Hutchison or written off as a loser whose face showed "drawn and bitter leanness" by Hugh MacLennan.[19]

Suddenly, Quebec sovereigntists were multiplying into a formidable force. And as they did so, Canadian commentary on Quebec lost the wistful tone that it had once possessed. Faced with the threat of its own dissolution, Canada suddenly remembered that there were two faces to romantic nationalism: one of them was warm and fuzzy and enjoyed step-dancing with the village girls.

But wasn't there another side? Hadn't romantic nationalism led to fascism, racism, and fanaticism in Europe? "The ambition of nationalists is to fuse the nation with the state [through] mystic commingling,"[20] said the *Globe and Mail* in a breathless editorial about the Parti Québécois last year, darkly adding that these are the sort of "people who believe they have a historic mission to fulfill."

Also, they're anti-Semites, added novelist Mordecai Richler in any forum that would publish him. Racists. Monsters, breathed the financial newspapers.

It was a remarkable transformation. In less than 30 years, English-Canadian rhetoric had changed from a nostalgic envy of Quebec to the diagnosis of a rapidly metastasizing fascist cancer on the banks of the St. Lawrence.

As always in these cases, the battle against nationalism itself generated nationalist behaviour. Seeing our country at risk, our civic nationalism is rapidly mutating back into the ethnic variety— ethnicity here defined in terms of language and territory. English-speaking Canadians are crying out, with appalling unanimity, that the 60 per cent of French-speaking Quebeckers who wish to secede are deluded and dangerous people who must be firmly dealt with. Many agree that fellow English speakers "trapped" within a seceding Quebec must be "saved," if necessary by sending the army to Montreal to forcibly keep it within Canada's boundaries. The nineteenth century provides several precedents for such "rescue missions," and they are invariably motivated by the majority's profound conviction of the inferiority of the seceding minority.[21]

"There is one type of fear more devastating than any other: the systemic fear that arises when a state begins to collapse," writes Michael Ignatieff. "Ethnic hatred is the result of the terror that arises when legitimate authority disintegrates."[22] Of course, he wasn't thinking of English Canadians when he wrote that. He was thinking of Serbians... or at least of Quebeckers.

Quebeckers themselves, however, were little intimidated by all of this. On the contrary, it confirmed their intuition that English Canada was not a place and English Canadians were not a people— just an agglomeration of confused and red-faced bullies. They had seen these bullies many times before, in the burning of the village of St. Denis, the schools of Saskatchewan, and the recruiting halls of the Canadian army, when new conscripts were told to choose between English or the brig.

Quebec has this advantage: it is older than English Canada, and has always been clear on the nature of its nationalism. The majority of thinkers in Quebec believe that a diffuse sentiment of being a "people" predates the Conquest by the English. In their view, the Conquest was a shock which caused this sentiment to become a conscious and "national" one.

It is perhaps not a coincidence that the word "nationalism" first appeared in an obscure German pamphlet published not many years after the Conquest, in 1774. Certainly it was an idea which seemed custom-made for the small and beleaguered "people" which had taken root by the shores of the St. Lawrence River.

CHAPTER TWO

"I hate melodrama," said Charles.

"It's all I love," said François.

"Can't we each write our version of the adventure?" continued Charles.

"A journal with two voices?"

"Exactly," replied Charles.

"That's ridiculous," said François. "You'd make a black accounting of our life, I'd paint it in neon."

— Jacques Godbout, *Les Têtes à Papineau*

Johann Gottfried Herder is not exactly a household name. He died in Weimar in 1803, and most of his books that can be found in the stacks of the McGill University library are in German, the preserve of philosophy students.

Yet Herder virtually invented the idea of nationalism. More precisely, as British philosopher Isaiah Berlin expresses it, Herder "invented the idea of belonging. He believed that just as people need to eat and drink, to have security and freedom of movement, so too they need to belong to a group. Deprived of this, they felt cut off, lonely, diminished, unhappy."[1]

Herder was born 16 years before the Conquest of Quebec in 1760. He was part of a great ferment of ideas that began at that time in Europe and that had to do with the self-determination of peoples— ironically at about the same time that the French in Canada lost theirs. A poignant aspect of Quebec's dilemma is that, while the fate of most of the nations that preoccupied Herder and his contemporaries was settled long ago, Quebec's purgatory has endured to the present day, a witness to the whole history of modern nationalism— while remaining, paradoxically, an instance of nineteenth-century romantic nationalism, preserved in aspic until the Quiet Revolution of the 1960's.

Herder was a student of Immanuel Kant. They lived during the remarkable period called the Enlightenment, when Europeans, who for long centuries had lived in submission to feudalism, finally declared the rights of mankind, and in particular the freedoms of the individual.

This was a time of exhilaration. But a number of thinkers were uneasy with mechanistic notions of man and nature. Could it really be possible that individuals were autonomous and self-creating, and human society little more than a useful device? They felt there was an aspect of the human spirit which required collective expression, but it was difficult to argue the case in this era predating sociology and psychology. All too often philosophers like Schelling were reduced to an appeal to intuition, to arguing that "individuals are only phantoms like the spectrum" and that "the freedom of the individual... lies in identifying himself with the whole."[2] The rationalists described such thinking as mysticism.

Kant tried to redress the matter by arguing that valuable knowledge could proceed from the close observation of human society. He called this "anthropology," and devoted a good part of his labour to it. He rejected the extremes of both individualism on the one hand and a collectivist élan vital on the other. He built a system "where the autonomy of the parts and the reality of the whole are not only reconciled but constitute [a] total solution: that of the person and the human community."[3]

Herder tried to maintain this balance, and made useful observations about the nature of the human individual. But his sympathies were with communities. Where Kant was reluctant to subdivide the community of all human beings, Herder proposed the startling idea that humanity is divided into a number of Volker, or peoples, each having "a set of customs and a life style, a way of perceiving and behaving that is of value solely because it is their own. The whole of cultural life is shaped from within the particular stream of tradition that comes of collective historical experience shared only by members of the group."[4] Such a people also had an organic relationship with the territory in which it lived, expressed even in its language.

Herder was— in effect— writing a critique of modernity, of an emerging world which in his view reduced men and women to "cultivated shadows." To him we owe the idea that human cultures have innate value and the right to survive. It is a "right" which cannot be enforced, and it is routinely pushed aside by the forces of technology and homogenization that are part of the triumphant modern world. It should not be surprising that these forces have sought to marginalize Herder's ideas, and to equate them with narrowness, exclusiveness, and fear of change.

Herder's real sin, however, was to celebrate human diversity and to oppose all forms of aggression by one people against another. This set him against the idea of "progress" and its corollary: that communities which resist progress can be, and indeed must be, pushed aside. However much his idea of "nationalism"— he invented the word— has lately come to be associated with intolerance of the Serbian variety, it must be remembered that for Herder, a society could not be "organic" unless it was also unaggressive.

For most of the past two centuries, Quebec has in many respects been a Herderian society. Incorporated into a powerful empire which was hostile to both its language and its religion, Quebec developed a strategy of survival (survivance) by turning inward on itself and nourishing its particular values.

But the difference between Quebec and the occupying British power was more profound even than language and religion: it was a difference over the nature of society itself. The British— and particularly Presbyterians with names like Molson and McGill— had been marked by the Calvinist idea that God has predestined certain human beings for salvation. Assiduous devotion to a worldly trade or calling, and the eschewing of leisure and pleasure, tended to prove that one was among the "elect." Poverty— or even a disinterest in business— on the other hand, tended to indicate that the person in question had been marked for damnation. This anathema could also be pronounced upon a society which seemed uninterested in commerce.

This gave rise to what Max Weber calls "those self-confident saints whom we can rediscover in the hard Puritan merchants of the heroic age of capitalism.[5] These were by no means restricted to England, but in England Puritan doctrine had shaken society more profoundly than elsewhere in Europe. Because one could not be certain who was among the elect, the virtuous person tended to hold himself apart from society and to mistrust the "friendship of men."[6] The whole notion of human community was placed in question, nowhere more so than in the writings of that Puritan-marked philosopher, John Locke. If Herder invented the idea of belonging, it was Locke who perfected the doctrine of solitude. He is the designer of the concept of the sovereign individual.

Today Locke is largely remembered for proclaiming a doctrine of human rights, especially freedom of speech and association. This he did, with no small courage, in the dark and despotic England of the 1680s and 1690s. What is less remembered— except by neo-conservative ideologues— is that Locke also argued that civil rights meant nothing unless private property were also secure. He went so far as to argue that civil rights were "possessions" that essentially resembled property.

This doctrine, which is called "possessive individualism," underlies North American materialism and can be seen in a debased form today in right-wing newspaper columnists who insist that consumerism— the right to consume— is the supreme expression of individual freedom.

By 1760 these ideas had shaken off some of their religious trappings and become a doctrine of secular behaviour, the so-called "Protestant work ethic." This is the belief that one should work more than necessary and accumulate more than one needs simply because a vague sort of virtue attaches to endless labour and self-aggrandizement. It was not a self-evident idea, this notion that "the sole purpose of [one's] life's work [is] to sink into the grave weighted down with a great material load of money and goods."[7] This doctrine was especially resisted in Catholic countries.

Thus the stage was set for that summer of 1760, when the great British fleet, its white sails dotting the St. Lawrence in a procession nearly 80 miles long, overthrew the French power in Canada. In the wake of that navy came a small horde of merchants intending to impose on Quebec an especially implacable world view. An early governor, James Murray, called them "licentious fanatics"— that is to say, people whose religion gave a moral coloration to what otherwise looked a good deal like greed. Murray became fond of what he saw as the opposing dignity and grace of French-Canadian society, and lobbied London to revoke the assimilationist Proclamation of 1763.

In histories such as Donald Creighton's *Empire of the St. Lawrence,* the Protestant merchants who offended Murray are much admired, while Murray is seen as a stiff and impractical aristocrat, a man as backward as the society of New France itself.

Creighton actually allied himself with the Lockeian argument, indirectly attacking the *other* profound current of modern history, that of Romanticism. "A series of disputes of this form runs through modern culture," writes McGill University philosopher Charles Taylor (although he was not particularly referring to the one I am using as an example here), "between what appear to be the demands of reason and disengaged freedom, and equality and universality, on one hand, and the demands of nature, or fulfillment, or expressive integrity, or intimacy, or particularity, on the other... the disputes... are all linked in some way or other to the great intramural debate of the last two centuries, pitting the philosophy of the Enlightenment against the various forms of Romantic opposition."[8]

Around this time, European countries were organizing themselves into nation states. People's allegiance to king, religion, and hierarchy was gradually being replaced with an allegiance to an abstract idea of "nation." But England developed a peculiar Calvinist variation of this idea. Here, "the individual was pre-eminent, the collective less important" than in other European countries.[9] This is the origin of the famous vagueness of British nationalism, later transferred to English Canada and much lamented by people like George Grant.

That is why histories such as *Empire of the St. Lawrence* (republished as late as 1956 and avidly read by the schoolchildren who now run English Canada), are not objective recountings, but rather jingoistic celebrations of "the struggle between insurgent commercial capitalism and a decadent and desperately resisting feudal and absolutist state"[10]— Quebec.

Creighton's association of vigour with the English and decadence with the French knew few limits. He approvingly quoted an anglophone Montreal newspaper at the time of the 1837 rebellions which claimed the French were infants "withering in the cradle in which they had been rocked."[11]

But Creighton was answered by equal fanaticism from the other side, in the voice of his Quebec contemporary, the priest, novelist and historian Lionel Groulx, who argued in an infamous novel called *L'Appel de la race* (1922)— translated as *The Iron Wedge*— that there must be separation of the French people from the empty materialism and prideful individualism of the English. Even a conservative historian like Ramsay Cook, himself not terribly sympathetic to Quebec, makes an equivalence between the extremists on each side: "For every Lionel Groulx, a Donald Creighton."[12]

Just as Donald Creighton was the spiritual heir of John Locke, so Lionel Groulx was, in a way, the heir and outcome of the ideas of Johann Herder. For the thing that needs to be observed about the pure ethnicity of Herder's ideal society is that no such place ever existed. It is an idea, come to replace the idea of the King, the Saviour, or the Great Chain of Being, older allegiances which had begun to shake and crumble in Europe as the peasants moved to the cities, became part of commercial society, and lost the simple rural virtues which Herder associated with an earlier and purer stage of humanity. "The savage who... glows with limited activity for his tribe as for his own life is, in my opinion, a more real being than that cultivated shadow [urban man]... The savage has room in his hut for every stranger. The deluged heart of the idle cosmopolite is a hut for no-one."[13]

This doctrine of clinging to the land and avoiding the corrupting city was used by the Catholic Church in nineteenth-century Quebec to lasting effect. It also underpinned the secular literary movement of the roman de la terre (novel of the land), of which the most famous was *Maria Chapdelaine*.

Herder was a great precursor of the Romantic movement, that humanist backlash against the excesses of liberal individualism. Like his contemporary Jean-Jacques Rousseau, Herder was not opposed to individualism per se, but asked how it could be reconciled with society. According to Charles Taylor, Herder actually helped define the modern individual by introducing the idea of uniqueness, that "there is a certain way of being human that is *my* way. I am called upon to live my life in this way, and not in imitation of anyone else's."[14]

It is ironic that the man who invented the idea of nationalism should also have contributed to the concept of the individual, but not contradictory. For Herder, there was no conflict between individual creativity and respect for a community's traditions. He felt that a healthy society reflected the creativity of individuals. This being the case, it is not surprising that Herder and other Romantic philosophers often expressed their ideas in artistic form. Rousseau's best-known book is a novel, *La Nouvelle Héloïse*, and when these ideas arrived in Quebec they were taken up by poets and novelists— a few of whom were also priests.

The Romantic idea is that the individual is primarily a creative unit rather than an economic or political one. This gave a powerful impetus to the movement of literary romanticism, in which poets often took on political roles, redeeming national languages that had been oppressed, or glorifying the new collectivity of the nation. The French were especially enthusiastic about this. Their great romantic poet, Lamartine, also became president of the republic. Others, like Alfred de Musset, were the inspiration of the founder-poets of Quebec nationalism, starting with Octave Crémazie in the 1850's.

The successors of Kant and Herder also developed a political expression of these ideas, and there the outcome was much more troubling. At the beginning of the 1800's, Germany existed only as a collection of principalities, which had been easily overrun by Napoleon's armies. Young intellectuals became obsessed with the idea that German culture could only be preserved within a powerful state. Schelling developed the view, according to Elie Kedourie, that such a state "is higher than the individual and comes before him." Fichte, the hard-liner, went further. In an aggressive world the state has not only the right but the *purpose* of applying "the surplus power of all its citizens for the furtherance of its own purposes."[15]

These ideas helped Bismarck to unify Germany, and their utility might well have ended there. But the late nineteenth century was an increasingly unstable place. "By the late 1880's in Europe, conservatives[16] saw in theories of ethnic purity and in the concept of race a barrier against the onslaught of an increasingly complicated and fragmenting world."[17] Even powerful capitalists found nationalism useful, calling for the erection of tariff barriers around the new nation states, the better to exploit something made possible only by defined borders and a customs system: a captive market.[18]

By the early twentieth century, nationalism was no longer associated simply with innocent but backward peoples trying to maintain their traditions. It had become the slogan of powerful nation states with undreamed-of powers to suppress and torment minority peoples.

This new, inflamed nationalism eventually made its way to Quebec, just as the earlier Romantic version had done. The inclusiveness of Louis-Joseph Papineau, who took shelter with a Jewish friend after the failure of the 1837 rebellion, was replaced with an ultramontane Catholic doctrine, both anti-English and anti-Semitic, that flourished among the Quebec intelligentsia from about 1900 to the beginning of World War II. There is no evidence that it had a wide popular following,[19] and quite a lot of evidence that it was a kind of imitative me-too-ism on the part of intellectuals who knew they were seen as marginal and ridiculous in North America, and therefore sought endorsement from Europe.

But never mind. Prominent Quebeckers had used ugly language, and English Canada would never let them forget it. Somehow in all this it is forgotten that Quebec was not in a position to commit the crimes which were committed in Europe, nor is there any evidence that it was inclined to do so.

There has been little violence in Canada, and more of it has been done by the federal government against Quebeckers than the other way around. It's not surprising, then, that the characteristic tone of Quebec nationalism has been peevish and resentful, rather than overbearing or violent. As Peter Alter has written, nationalism has been a rallying cry of both aggressive nations and genuinely oppressed ones. "It can be associated with forces striving for... emancipation, as well as with those whose goal is oppression."[20]

Because Quebec's emancipation struggle has been going on for such a very long time, it has become a sort of museum piece of Herderian nationalism. Herder's defenders, including Isaiah Berlin, insist that his philosophy has no racial content. He "said nothing about race and nothing about blood. He only spoke about soil, language, common memories and customs."[21] Indeed, he was not the first to draw this distinction. Two-and-a-half thousand years ago, the rhetorician Isocrates, in attempting to build a pan-Hellenic federation, observed that "the people we call Greeks are those who have the same culture as ours, not the same blood."[22] Since World War II, this has also been the vocabulary of Quebec nationalism, which defines "Québécitude" as a willingness to live in French and to regard Quebec as one's homeland. There are few if any references to race as a criterion of belonging.

Since the Holocaust, however, doctrinaire liberals have insisted that it is not possible to draw a line between cultural nationalism and racism. A persuasive exponent of this viewpoint is Elie Kedourie, who, in a classic study of nationalism written in 1960, argues that nationalism is different from the patriotism which people have always felt. Nationalism, "far from being a universal phenomenon, is a product of European thought in the last 150 years."[23]

Answering Herder's description of an organic society where social solidarity is maintained by the suppleness of a common language, Kedourie retorts: How can a people live together for a long time in a closed environment, resisting outside influence, without thinking of themselves as a race? "There [can be] no definite clear-cut distinction between linguistic and racial nationalism."[24]

These two views of cultural nationalism strongly influence English Canada's view of Quebec and Quebec's view of itself. In Quebec's narrative, for example, the dominant historians, led by Michel Brunet, speak of the Conquest as a trauma which destroyed a happy and whole people who had taken root by the banks of the St. Lawrence River. They were "decapitated" of their adminstrative and merchant class, which was deported, and required generations to recover.

In this view, Quebeckers were aware of themselves as a people from the beginning, even *before* nationalist dogmas reached them[25]— that is, they were an instance of a Herderian people— and one can trace their history of resistance to English domination from 1760 to the present.

"What is nationalism?" writes Brunet. "It is simply the manifestation of the natural and spontaneous solidarity that exists among members of a human group sharing a historical and cultural tradition from which the group derives its distinctive identity." Since "acting and thinking collectively" is a necessity for human beings, nationalism "is not an ideology."[26]

In these histories it is argued that the Canadiens believed that Canada would continue to be a French-speaking country under British rule. When the British reduced the French to a minority and the English Canadians restricted them to a "reserve" in Quebec, a betrayal occurred which can only be reversed by political independence.

In these retellings, the English are sometimes represented neutrally, as having yielded in a human way to the temptation of exploiting their advantage; but quite often it is suggested that they were racists, or very close to it.

Those who resisted them, of course, take on a heroic quality in most of these narratives. "The Canadiens, mere playthings of adverse forces which overwhelmed them, entered into national conflict with the new English colonization of the Laurentian valley," says a book published last year. "Certainly, an indestructible survivance [struggle of the soul] was quickly imposed upon the French Canadians."[27] Essayists such as Christian Dufour turn over the minutest stones of history in order to show the continuing effect of the Conquest on the behaviour of both the English and the French.

A corollary of the francophone view is that English Canada lacks an identity. "A hundred and thirty years after Confederation, the Canadian state and constitution are supported by popular national sovereignty, but without fully constituting the idea of a people or of a nation."[28]

Finally, to the practical argument that Quebec was better off under progressive British rule, Brunet replies: "A people has the right to remain poor, backward and underdeveloped. They even have the right to idealize their mediocrity and convince themselves that they are an example of values superior to those of other societies... if [this people] lives on an island lost in the ocean, free of competition with other nations, its situation, however unhappy, does not condemn it to submit without defense to the domination of another people."[29] Here Brunet argues, following Herder, that cultures have a right to survive. Even a culture that is demonstrably richer or more efficient than its neighbour does not therefore acquire the right to impose itself.

I became aware of the answering English-Canadian orthodoxy in 1995, when I wrote an article which argued that Quebec nationalism is a rooted phenomenon and that English Canada must engage it.[30] I quoted a snippet of Dufour to support this contention.

Within three days, an answering article[31] was submitted by Ramsay

Cook, professor of history at York University, whose prolific output includes a book on nationalism in Canada. His argument was that the Conquest was a battle between two foreign armies which, to the habitants, amounted to little more than exchanging one master for another. It had no lasting effects. Since then Canada has gradually recognized the moral rights of the French language in law. The capstone of this recognition was the language and education provisions of Pierre Trudeau's Charter of Rights and Freedoms.

Cook added that it is false to think the French in Canada have any basis on which to claim independence. Nationalism *is* (pace Brunet) an ideology. Those sympathetic to such claims are "wrong-headed," engaged in a "quest for power," and a clear danger to those outside their ethnic group. This is, I think, an admirable summation of the extreme liberal viewpoint as espoused by Pierre Trudeau: there are only individual rights, and any kind of collective right is of necessity a threat to the freedom of all.

As with Kedourie, this logic insists that no line can be drawn between ethnic nationalism and racism. It is not surprising, then, to read another prominent historian, Kenneth McNaught, arguing in a 1966 article that "the whole concept of two nations is false," and that to even conceive of such a thing is to sanction "racial nations." McNaught was frank enough to add that "there was never any question of an 'equality of two founding races'" and that, in our constitution, "the 'races' were, in fact, not equal."[32]

McNaught is the author of the history of Canada which I studied in high school.

On both sides, of course, there have been dissidents. Charles Taylor argued long ago that French Canadians are, by any reasonable definition of the term, a historical "people." As long ago as 1960, Mason Wade noted in tongue-in-cheek fashion that upwellings of Quebec nationalism usually provoke the following anglophone reaction: "'Was it not true, as had often been whispered, that French Canada was fascist at heart, totalitarian, authoritarian, and had no real instinct for North American democracy or for the Anglo-Saxon tradition?' Such remarks were often heard, and they were not offset by any real intermingling of the races at any social or political level."[33]

Admirable scholars, such as Arthur Lower in the 1946 classic *Colony to Nation*, tried to encourage English Canadians to understand the impact of the Conquest, but despaired that they would ever do so:

> It is hard for people of English speech to understand the feelings of those who must pass under the yoke of conquest, for there is scarcely a memory of it in all their tradition. Conquest is a type of slavery and of that too they have no memory, except as masters. Conquest, like slavery, must be experienced to be understood... the life-structure of the conquered is laid open to their masters. Wherever they turn, something meets their eyes to symbolize their subjection. It need not be the foreign military... it may be some quite small matter: a common utensil of unaccustomed size and shape, let us say, taking the place of a familiar one.[34]

Some of these dissidents were at one time prominent, and remain eloquent, but their ideas were non-existent in the Canadian media in the two years leading up to the referendum. In fact, there was little discussion of Canadian history in the thousands of referendum stories. Many of them, however, took care to let out a strident whoop and a belly laugh at the idea that Quebec had been "humiliated" in Confederation. Jack McLeod, a retired political scientist of the University of Toronto, says that "the Trudeau orthodoxy is so strong that most of us who disagree don't even bother sending articles to the newspapers. They aren't printed."[35]

On the French side, there was a strong dissident reaction to the Brunet "decapitation" idea. Fernand Ouellet was able to demonstrate that there had not been extensive deportation, and that in fact not much of a middle class existed in New France in 1760. He also said that the perfidious

Protestant merchants weren't as bad as myth has it, and that if the French merchants ended up poorer after the arrival of the English, it was pretty much their own fault.

The rhetorical tone of the older generation of contemporary Quebec writers also seems to grate on the nerves of the younger generation. There is, in Quebec, a general fatigue with the cult of self-pity.

One example of this reaction is a droll book, *Du Canada au Québec,* written in 1987 by psychologist Heinz Weinmann, a kind of history of Quebec's post-Conquest feeling sorry for itself. An example he particularly enjoys is Philippe Aubert de Gaspé's classic 1863 novel, *Les anciens canadiens.* In this woeful tale, Quebec is an infant abandoned to Albion by the French motherland. "A sombre veil covered all of New France," writes de Gaspé, "for the mother country, en vraie marâtre [a really wicked stepmother], had abandoned her Canadian children!"[36]

Taking note of how quickly the views of Fernand Ouellet were marginalized within history faculties, Weinmann argues (tongue-in-cheek) that history is about storytelling, and Ouellet writes a dull novel. "Needless to say, Fernand Ouellet has few disciples in Quebec! People have little use for this economic perspective on history... Ouellet and his followers, if he has any, are ostracized because he postulates a continuing road exactly where one needs to see a trench..."[37]

English and French Canada telling the story of Quebec! It's like listening to competing storytellers reciting different texts while trying to gouge each other's eyes out. A similar image inspired Jacques Godbout's novel *Les Têtes à Papineau* (Papineau's Heads), published the year after the 1980 referendum. In this tale, Charles and François are two heads on the same body. As it happens, Charles speaks good English, while François prefers French. They have managed somehow to grow to adulthood, the one discreetly closing his eyes while the other makes love to his girlfriend, the other answering the questions during TV interviews.

But they've grown tired of bifurcation, and have agreed to a radical surgery which will fuse their heads together. The doctor is, of course, an anglophone who believes that technology can fix anything. "Dr. Northridge wouldn't do anything to hurt us. He's aware we each have our view of things. He doesn't want to annihilate us... in reality he believes that if the operation succeeds we'll be happier. Happy."[38]

Humour is a frequent francophone response to the intolerable pressure of English-speaking culture— the "other head" which is always right there beside you, always talking, rarely listening. The notion that two cultures that don't speak each other's languages can fuse into something called "national unity" doesn't make much sense to anybody who stops to think about it. Francophones think about it a good deal, which seems to be the reason they, and not English Canadians, write novels like *Les Têtes à Papineau*.

Before the two heads, there was the Arcadian period, lasting 152 years between the founding of New France in 1608 and the Conquest. If a "people" in the sense intended by the nationalist philosophers ever existed in Quebec, it would have come into existence at this time.

But the habitants, most of them illiterate, have left little record of who they thought they were. "Nothing is harder than studying the influence of the habitant on culture. It's evident in the adaptation of living quarters, food and clothing to the new conditions... but how to measure the 'mentalités'?"[39]

Enough documentation about them exists, however, to let both English- and French-speaking historians tell their external story with a certain degree of unanimity (which agreement abruptly ends in 1760 with the Conquest).

Most agree that the early society was marked by the Catholic mysticism of the founders, who were financed by aristocrats in the grip of a religious revival. The French government of the day refused to allow Protestants to settle in New France, giving the colony its homogeneous Catholic complexion and ensuring the people would not actually meet or know those of other faiths. A century-and-a-half later, in 1766, a British official noted that the habitants still "regard all Protestants with an eye of hatred."[40]

However— and this is the beginning of a series of paradoxes that must be kept in mind— the actual Catholicism practised by the habitants was not very rigorous. There were never enough priests to monitor the far-flung parishes, and marriages were often common-law. The people "domesticated the Catholic religion and used it for their own purposes,"[41] primarily ceremonial, to mark the seasons and social events.

Also, while puritanism developed in England and France at about the same time, the French variety was less virulent. "Unlike the Puritans of Massachusetts Bay, who had set themselves the task [of reforming] all Christendom, the clergy and their lay followers of New France set modest goals... thereby sparing themselves much frustration."[42] This Jansenist puritanism "didn't prevent the people of New France from living with an appearance of fecklessness that impressed visiting Europeans,"[43] writes George Woodcock.

French puritanism was not directed against sexuality, leading to a surprising candour and absence of self-consciousness of which sociologist Marcel Rioux sees the traces in a village he studied, where "sexual activity, without being erotic, was numerous and varied. I had the impression of witnessing a natural and not at all anxious sexuality."[44] Most English Canadians who live in modern Quebec can't help noticing this particular cultural difference. Indeed, it's hard to pry some of them away from it.

There was also genetic homogeneity. France was not a successful colonizer, and only managed to send about 10,000 mostly Norman settlers to Quebec before the Conquest. But these few had an enormously high birth rate, encouraged not so much by the Church as by the infinite availability of land. These were the ancestors of most of the millions of francophones in North America today, making that population "homogeneous to a degree entirely alien to the Anglo-Saxon imagination."[45]

The French government was the most centralized in Europe, with the intendant system linking "every region of France... to the monarchy"[46]— including New France. But the system was well-administered and benign, with a host of intermediaries, many of them locally appointed so that "every individual could eventually find a sense of communal belonging."[47] In Quebec, this meant that most of the officials and intermediaries were Quebeckers, not Frenchmen.

Because the settlers "had few direct ties with France, their economic existence, their peculiar mores, virtually everything in their lives was firmly rooted in Canada."[48] As early as 1664, a certain P. Boucher wrote that "when I stayed in Paris last year I met several easeful persons who had been Habitants de nostre Canada, and who had left it on account of the war, who assured me that they were impatient to return: so much does la Nouvelle-France have something *attractive* for those who know how to taste its sweetness."[49] By 1680, the majority of New France's population had been born there.

The seigneurial system of land tenure, where each farm had frontage on the St. Lawrence River, encouraged people to stay physically close together. "There was little scattering in all directions," writes Arthur Lower. "It was favourable to communal life. The habitant never really abandoned society, as so many English settlers did."[50]

However, an accident of history gave this tightly knit society an extraordinary opening into a larger world: at its back door lay an unexplored continent. Heinz Weinmann illustrates the effect by looking at the earliest maps where two Canadas were marked. The first is a narrow strip of settled territory along the river between Quebec and Montreal; but the second Canada is "written in large letters the length of the St. Lawrence. This Canada already had no end, no limits. Like a vector, it not so much covers the area of a territory as it indicates a direction: the route of penetration of Canada... which opens on the Pays d'en Haut."[51]

Some seigneurs complained about how hard it was to keep young men on the farms when they could run off into the woods and become coureurs de bois. Here they formed trading relationships with the natives, whose languages they learned to speak. Those natives were also present in the towns and villages, and items of their clothing and habits were borrowed by the settled farmers. Shocked Europeans noticed that habitant women, when working, pulled up their skirts and tucked them into their belts, leaving their legs bare as native women did. By 1683, the habitants were already calling themselves Canadiens, a name borrowed from the natives. "Any assimilation in this first century of French colonization of America, passed from civilized toward native"; that is, the Canadiens were influenced by the natives rather than the other way around.[52]

The continental French were as racist as any Europeans at the time. Champlain left journals full of the usual derogatory remarks about "savages." But the habitants, acting as intermediaries between the natives and the French traders, no longer thought of *themselves* as French. They were a separate, and small, society which had to get along with the much more numerous indigenous people.

This led to an astute observation by Pierre de Charlevoix in 1710, comparing the attitudes of the habitants with the British settlers farther south. "The British-Americans do not humour the savages, because they see no need to do so. [But] the French youth... get along well with the natives, whose friendship they always earn."[53]

This is not to overlook the bloody battles which took place with the Iroquois, or the aggressiveness of the missionaries, any more than it is to overlook the racial tensions of Oka or Kahnesetake today. But during a prolonged period where they were few in numbers and vulnerable— a period which had no counterpart in the English settlement of the continent— the Canadiens learned an acceptance of the indigenous peoples.

Peter Kalm, a Dutch traveller, wrote in 1749 that he was relieved to arrive in Quebec. "The people here [in Quebec] are much more polite than the people in the English provinces."[54] But not self-effacing. As the Baron Lahontan expressed it in 1731, the Canadiens "regard themselves as above all the nations of the earth."[55] On the content of these records, historians of both languages today can agree. But one need only ask, *Were these Canadiens a "people"?* and the fracture appears.

Laval University sociologist Fernand Dumont, an assiduous scholar and long-time separatist, argues in his 1993 book *La Genèse de la société québécoise* that all of the above factors combined to give Quebeckers not only an identity, but a consciousness of that identity. "One can speak in this sense of a 'national sentiment,' of the sort we see with other peoples far back in history and which I would freely describe as archaic... This sentiment was certainly present in New France."[56]

This description, particularly the word "archaic," puts Dumont in the Herderian tradition. It is very difficult to find an English-speaking historian to agree with it.

In fact, non-Quebec historians find the evident happiness of this society, and its good relations with the French government, proof of the contrary. W.J. Eccles argued in 1974 that nationalism is usually created by brutal repression, as was the case in the Spanish colonies. The people in New France were well-treated by the French monarchy. "Without grievances, social friction, propaganda and direction from above, the virus of nationalism could not take hold."[57]

This is a note often sounded by anglophone historians, even sympathetic ones like Eccles. He provides the reason why:

French-Canadian historians can hardly be blamed for treating the Conquest as a disaster, yet English Canadians sometimes regard that attitude as suspect, if not seditious. English-Canadian historians tend, either expressly or as an unstated and perhaps unconscious premise, to regard the outcome of the struggle as having been inevitable, since *had it been different their world would not exist today*, which is unthinkable.[58]

CHAPTER THREE

Et dis-moi maintenant, de ta voix satanique,

Qui vont pouvoir flétrir par sa verve cynique

Dans un libelle atroce, ignoble, révoltant

L'histoire que tout bon Français aimait tant;

Et qui savait si bien, o gallant troubadour,

En huant— Jeanne d'Arc chanter la Pompadour!

Dis-moi, de cette voix tant de fois sacrilège,

Ce qui valait pourtant QUELQUES ARPENTS DE NEIGE.

Say unto me now, with your satanic voice

Whose cynical verve, in a satire of choice—

Atrocious! Revolting!— will wither a past

Whose pages the noblest Frenchmen once blessed...

And who knew, oh so well, you gallant troubador

—Joan of Arc being judged by the whore Pompadour!—

Oh tell me! like those priests who have felt your tongue's blow

What's the price, to the nickel, of A FEW ACRES OF SNOW?

— Louis Fréchette attacks Voltaire, *La Légende d'un peuple*

It is a truism that "nothing stimulates a national identity more than adversity."[1] The trauma of being conquered— that is, not just beaten on the battlefield, but permanently occupied— is capable of causing a literary renaissance by itself.

This is what occurred in Quebec. However, it wasn't the Conquest of 1760 that provoked the birth of imaginative fiction. Rather, it was the long-delayed aftermath, the Rebellion of 1837, after which the British made the fateful decision to forcibly assimilate the French Canadians by amalgamating their province with English-speaking Upper Canada. For galvanizing a culture to defend itself, this is the best possible kind of threat.

From the British point of view, both the ruthlessness of the 1840 Act of Union and the relative benignness of the Conquest were logical. The earlier struggle had led to no formal reprisals against the Canadiens because they were not really combatants: the battle at that time was between England and France. But in 1837 it was clearly the Canadiens, alone and unaided, who had taken up arms against British soldiers. Even worse, they had done so employing the language of the romantic national uprisings which were beginning to shake the European continent. Their charismatic leader, Louis-Joseph Papineau, evoked the French Revolution by encouraging people to wear "French liberty caps" and to "melt their spoons to make bullets."[2] Worse, Papineau called on them to defend their language and religion from an alien people— the English.

Once the rebellion was crushed, London sent one of the outstanding political minds of the time, James Durham, to solve the underlying dilemma. But it was an unfortunate decision, because Lord Durham was a man torn between the individualist creed of England and the Continent's Romantic ideas. He measured the French in Canada against both ideologies, and found them twice deficient.

It was Durham the romantic, handsome in a soulful and dark-eyed way, who, coming ashore in Quebec City, "mounted a great white charger and, his retinue behind him, rode in solemn state to the Castle of St. Louis."[3] The beauty of Durham's wife had inspired Byron to write a love poem shortly before Byron went off to die in the war for Greek independence.

It is not surprising, then, that the death sentence Durham pronounced against French culture in North America was justified in the first instance by artistic criteria. "They are a people without a history and without a literature," he wrote, adding for good measure that "cut off from every people that speaks to its own language [the French Canadians] can support no national stage."[4]

There is even evidence that he was familiar with Fichte's ideas about language. "Those who have reflected on the powerful influence of language on thought, will perceive in how different a manner people who think in different languages are apt to think... the same opinion... expressed by an English and a French writer [is] so diferent as to mark utterly different habits of thought." He added that so long as "no large portion of the community can read both languages with ease" the newspapers of each would misrepresent the views of the other. This would lead to "gross delusions"[5] on both sides.

Then, to administer the coup de grâce, we hear from Durham the successful aristocrat-businessman. He understood that the traditional economy of New France gave its people a comfortable living, but predicted that they could not compete with the cyclone of Protestant free enterprise which the English had unleashed in North America and would finish up as labourers in the employ of English capitalists.

The French had failed both as a community (according to romantic standards) and as individuals (according to Lockeian individualism). They deserved, in Durham's opinion, to perish.

The political steps taken to suppress the French after the Durham Report appeared in 1839 were draconian, but short-lived because of widespread popular resistance. An edict that English only would be spoken in the new Legislature, for example, led to the election of a flood of Quebec deputies who could not speak a syllable of the language.[6]

By 1848 the assimilation policy was dead, and the rebellion leaders who had not been hanged were pardoned. But it was too late. A formidable writer named François-Xavier Garneau had been provoked to answer Durham's annihilating remarks by creating both a history and a literature in Quebec. In the four years after 1845 he wrote a four-volume history which set out to prove to the Canadiens that they were a people with a story as telling and dramatic as that of any other people. Garneau admitted that Quebec still lacked a literature, but called upon young writers to fill the gap.

This young literature was at first one of reaction. Garneau himself, the poet Louis Fréchette, and even the gentle novelist Philippe Aubert de Gaspé were filled with "an immense disappointment" and a "sentiment of exile"[7] after the failure of the rebellion. But there was also anger, as much with France for abandoning Quebec as with the English for colonizing it.

Anger can spark good writing; more importantly, it sparks a sense of self, a prise de conscience. Consider Garneau, at the time an unknown journalist, deciding to assault Voltaire— then as now a towering figure of European culture— for having counselled Louis XVI that Canada was "a few acres of ice and snow" not worth keeping. The Quebecker imagines Voltaire throwing a party to celebrate the loss of Quebec to the British where, almost seditiously, he entertains his guests with a pro-British play called *The Insular Patriot*. Voltaire himself plays the lead.

> After the performance the windows of the gallery flew open, and the guests looked out upon a spacious court illuminated and ornamented with savage trophies. To the strains of martial music a great display of fireworks was ignited. Rockets were fired from a gigantic St. George's Cross, above which one could make out a representation of the Cataracts of Niagara.[8]

Whether or not this explosion of high kitsch (unmentioned by French historians) really happened is beside the point. Garneau was writing literature, and the episode was a fable whose lesson was not lost on his readers: neither England nor France had Quebec's interests at heart. Quebeckers must save themselves, and in order to do that, they must invent themselves.

The first Quebec novel, *L'Influence d'un livre*, had already appeared in 1837. But it was a fantastical work with folkloric overtones which made no overt reference to the political situation. That changed, however, with the appearance of the first roman du terroir (novel of the land) in 1846. In *La terre paternelle,* Patrice Lacombe tells the story of a family that sells its farm to an Englishman. The older son, a coureur de bois who knew nothing about the transaction, returns home years later and finds a stranger living there. "What business brings you here?" demands the new owner, in English. "I'm sorry, sir," replies the son [in French], "but I don't speak English very well."[9] And the conversation continues, with the Englishman speaking broken French.

The son eventually buys back the farm, restoring both order and happiness. This plot was the first instance of a pattern which would be repeated in countless novels during the next 100 years. In these stories the French-Canadian countryside is an earthly paradise. Into this blessed place comes an Englishman, often a greedy and underhanded one; or else, as in the famous novel *Jean Rivard* (1862, reprinted 18 times) a new parish is founded from which English Protestants are excluded.

A final variant is seen in the most famous roman du terroir of all, where *Maria Chapdelaine* (1914) resists the temptation to emigrate to the bright lights of the American city. Maria knows that life would be better there, but in a mystic vision she hears the "voice of Quebec" urging her to stay and make new children to ensure the survival of the French-Canadian people.

Underlying these novels is a profound alienation from the political process. The image of retreating to the countryside is related to the powerful myth of the Sleeping Beauty, where a people is "pricked by external forces of evil and put to sleep until the nationalist dawn arrives to restore the community."[10] In the French-Canadian variant, Quebec is in the hands of an occupying power, and the strategy for survival is to fall back on the final redoubt: the parish. If this little social unit can be made economically self-sufficient (the second half of *Jean Rivard* is subtitled "Jean Rivard, Economist") then the religion and the culture can survive the dark age of outside occupation.

Did the "Englishman" really deserve this opprobrium? Not in the literal sense. Although there were certainly bigots among the British merchants and settlers, they did not deserve to be compared with disguised devils (as happened in another novel, *Charles Guérin*, published in 1853). But to imagine that the novelists intended these descriptions to be taken literally (as writer William Johnson did in his 1991 book *Anglophobie: Made in Quebec*) is to misunderstand the way literature works.

What happened in this literature is that the writers attempted to dramatize the threat of assimilation. The more sophisticated realized that individual English settlers were not malicious and probably were not even aware of the cultural threat posed by their presence. But the threat was nonetheless real, and dramatizing it often meant embodying it in the story's (English-speaking) villain.

In English-language commentary on Quebec there is a tendency to argue that the cultural nationalism which flared up after 1837 is a concocted phenomenon. If it was real, it is argued, why did it not appear soon after the original Conquest?

One possible answer is that "the traumatic effects of the Conquest... reduced [Quebec's] people to silence and withdrawal."[11] The educated minority could see the coming repression in arbitrary decisions, such as that of a British judge who decided in 1825 that all trials would be in English even if the defendants could not understand the language. But the large labouring population was only aware of a vague discomfort in the presence of the English, who "stood for restlessness, change, a striving after wealth... a kind of bearish individualism."[12]

The first French-language newspaper, *Le Canadien*, was founded in 1806, and contained a confusing range of opinions. "Canadien, chéris dans ton coeur/L'union qui fait ton bonheur/Bénis la Providence,/Qui voulant par le doux lien,/Fixer à jamais ton destin,/T'a soustrait à la

France," wrote one correspondent that year: "Canadien, cherish the union which brings happiness; bless Providence, which wishing by a sweet link [to England] to fix forever your destiny, has removed you from France."[13]

By way of foreshadowing the divisions of contemporary Canada, one writer advocated that "the English here should no longer think of themselves as English, nor the Canadiens think of themselves as French" but both should fuse into "a people."[14] Another, however, replied in proto-nationalist terms that "our geographic position destines us to form a people entirely different from the French and even from our [American] neighbours. The nature of our soil, our needs and our agriculture, will necessarily create a marked difference between our mores and those of other peoples."[15]

This confusion existed in private life as well. At a French house party in 1808 a lady in from the country is baffled at the presence of two young "Englishmen." She "asked who these men were," writes the host. "I replied, blushing somewhat, that one of them was the son of her cousin. 'But how is it that they only speak English?' she asked. 'Don't they know their own language?'" The host replies, still embarrassed, that it is a fashion. "Our young people like to exercise themselves to speak English."[16]

Hubert Aquin, the great separatist novelist who committed suicide in 1977, often wrote about "the attraction the colonizer's values and culture have for the colonized people, who suffer from an imposed 'amnesia' following their conquest."[17]

The amnesia, however, began to dissipate in the 1820's with the arrival of the new idea of organic or cultural nationalism from Europe. The thinking of Herder and Rousseau had fused into an influential doctrine which seemed the perfect solution to the problems of the little population— now grown to about a half-million— on the shores of the St. Lawrence.

Nobody denies that these ideas arrived in Quebec at about that time, but once again there is an important difference in the way that English and French-speaking writers today evaluate their impact. English-Canadian historians, for example, argue that these concepts were adopted by a frustrated intellectual minority of francophones who spread them among an ignorant rural population. This perspective is evidently that of the Kedourie school, to the effect that nationalism was strictly a nineteenth-century phenomenon, and often the work of mischievous intellectuals.

Most French-Canadian scholars, on the other hand, make a Herderian argument that nationalist ideas merely gave the Quebec people a vocabulary with which to describe a felt reality.

The gulf can be illustrated by looking at the work of Susan Trofemik-off, an anglophone historian, and Fernand Dumont, a francophone sociologist who is also a nationalist.

Trofemikoff, although sympathetic to Quebec, is suspicious of the early stirrings of nationalism. She notes that "a new ideological and popular force emanating from [France's] European neighbours"[18] reached Quebec in the 1820's. It found fertile ground in a growing francophone middle class that was cut off from English-dominated commerce.

> Without the economic base to bolster its social and political ambitions, the middle class turned to something for which its education had prepared it— an ideology. The principle of nationalities, imported from Europe and sounding like liberalism, could make a people look like an individual... How simple then to distinguish French Canadians by their language, their religion, their social institutions. And how pleasant to name oneself their spokesman.[19]

In this retelling, the French-speaking bourgeoisie was an idle, somewhat pompous chattering class which was reading a little too much Kant and Herder for its own good. The Parti Canadien which it founded was not "as ethnically pure as its name implied" and when it later changed its name to the Parti Patriote, it was "advertising its nationalist pretensions."

Fernand Dumont also notes the arrival in Quebec of "the nationalities movement which agitated Europe."[20] But in his version of the story there is no mischievous local bourgeoisie. Rather, this new doctrine of "the people as an entity formed in a concrete way by history, that is, as a nation"[21] served as a "stimulant" to the whole French-Canadian population of the 1830's.

In his view, the Canadiens already had an "archaic" sort of "national sentiment," and the British themselves had inflamed it by reiterating the inferiority of the French and forcing the latter to justify their existence as a people.[22] This places Dumont in the camp of thinkers like Isaiah Berlin, who argues the "bent twig" theory of nationalism: that a national identity can be obscured for a time by an occupying power, but it will snap back as soon as an opportunity presents itself.

By the early 1850's, only a few nationalist novels had been written, but a literary salon had already formed in the back room of a Quebec City bookshop run by a would-be poet named Octave Crémazie. François-Xavier Garneau was often there, as was the young poet Louis Fréchette, and the superintendent of public instruction, Pierre-Joseph Olivier Chauveau, a future premier of Quebec and the author of the novel *Charles Guérin*.

Poets like Crémazie and Fréchette, in the view of critic George Woodcock, established a tradition that was immediately "more interesting" than that of the early English-Canadian poets, because "they show at least the passionate resentment of a people anxious to redress the humiliation"[23] inflicted on them by an outside power. They would perform an alchemy on nationalist ideas, transforming them into literary expression that influences Quebeckers to the present day.

Also present in Crémazie's bookshop, and rather more ominously, was the Abbé Henri-Raymond Casgrain, who, like most of the senior clergy of the Catholic Church, was taking a very great interest in this literary revival.

The position of the Church vis-à-vis British Protestant rule had always been ambiguous. After the Conquest it had been a struggle to get permission to name a new bishop, and he was not officially recognized until 1818. The number of priests dropped vertiginously until the 1830's,[24] and the people remained, as they always had been, charmingly delinquent about religious observance.

When the nationalist movement began to take shape, things got worse. The young professionals who led it were fond of French and American ideas, which meant they were anti-clerical.[25] The Church defended itself by underlining its loyalty to the British government and extending its control over education.

The Rebellion of 1837 was the deciding moment. When it was crushed, the bishop of Montreal immediately reminded the British governor of the clergy's loyalty. Acting on another front, the brilliant Monsignor Bourget proposed a new church structure where "there will be unity of conduct by all the bishops of the province, and greater majesty and pomp in religious observance"[26] so that the government would think twice before threatening it. This was the beginning of the bejewelled green-eyed monster of Quebec clerical Catholicism.

The liberal nationalists were momentarily crushed by Lord Durham's report and its call for assimilation. Both military and political resistance had proven futile. What was left? In 1839 their intellectual leader, the journalist Étienne Parent, wrote that the French must not "struggle foolishly against the inflexible course of events... without doubt it would have been sweet to live and die in the hope of keeping alive the nationality of our fathers on the shores of the St. Lawrence... it is this hope that we must abandon. Assimilation will be accomplished gradually and without unpleasantness..."[27]

The liberals did not give up immediately, however. In fact, they re-organized as a political party, the Rouges, and founded l'Institut canadien de Montréal in 1844, a library and conference centre dedicated to liberal freedoms.

Their enemy by now, however, was not so much the British but the newly powerful Catholic Church which insisted, among other things, on censoring the Institut's library. Before the struggle was over, prominent members of the Institut had been excommunicated, and the Institut itself shut down.

But it is important to remember that the liberals were also cultural nationalists.

They were caught in an insufferable vise grip. Weakened by the uprising, many of their leaders dead, they were now fighting not only the British government but also their own religion. And although they were attracted by the civic ideals of the French revolution, they knew that the survival of the French in Canada would depend on cultural unanimity, "with unity of language, customs, religion, laws and institutions which composed the Canadian nationality," said their newspaper, *L'Avenir*[28]— adding to the list of criteria for a "people" one that the nationalist philosophers had scrupulously avoided: "religion."

It was religion that finally finished the Rouge liberals, even to the extent of shutting down the newspaper *L'Avenir*. Its editor, Jean-Baptiste-Éric Dorion, was so discouraged that he literally retreated to the woods, buying virgin land and founding a village. This inspired Antoine Gérin-Lajoie's 1862 novel *Jean Rivard*, the tale of a strapping young man who buys a piece of wilderness and surrounds himself with friends who soon create a prosperous village. Significantly, Jean Rivard's best friend is the Church's local emissary, the priest Octave Doucet. They create a tiny— but undemocratic— utopia.

The tone of the novel is not anti-English. Rivard buys his land from an English speculator, but at a fair price; and some Irish Catholics come to live in his village. Later on he is elected to Parliament, but arrives in Montreal only shortly before an enraged mob of anglophones burns Parliament to the ground in 1849 for daring to vote compensation to people whose property was damaged during the 1837 rebellion.

This was one of the most hateful episodes of anglophone bigotry in Canadian history, but Jean Rivard does not have an unkind word for the English. Hovering at a great height above the political fray, he observes merely that cities breed strife and contestation. He returns to his village in the woods, determined to make it economically self-supporting. Nearby is a lovely lake which he has named Lamartine, after the French romantic poet.

Gérin-Lajoie had been, in the 1830's, one of the most fiercely anti-clerical of the young nationalists. *Jean Rivard* represents his capitulation to the church, and he was not by any means alone in this capitulation.

To return, then, to Octave Crémazie's bookshop. Crémazie is remembered today as Quebec's first national poet (a half-century before Émile Nelligan), but he was a strange mixture of qualities. Nationalist but not separatist, a lover of Quebec but not of the land (there is almost nothing about nature in his poetry), Crémazie had a morbid fascination with heroism and death.

In the discouraging aftermath of the Durham Report, when tough leaders like Étienne Parent were ready to give up, Crémazie "contributed to the stiffening of Canadien resolve without which the Act of Union would have had disastrous consequences."[29] At a time when many demoralized Canadiens planned to flee to the United States, Crémazie lyricized the idea that a deep and satisfying life can only be lived in one's homeland.

Quand vous auriez de l'or les faveurs adorées/ Ces biens rempliraient-ils vos ames altérées?/ Il nous faut quelque chose dans cette triste vie/ Qui... nous éleve au-dessus de la realité... C'est le ciel du pays, le village natal/Loin de son lieu natal l'insensé qui s'exile/ Il n'a devant les yeux le ciel de la patrie/ Et le sol sous ses pas n'a point de souvenirs.

When you have the favours of gold, will your altered soul be fulfilled? We need something in this sad life to lift us above reality... the sky of our country, the village where we were born. The madman who exiles himself far from these things no longer sees his country's sky, and the ground beneath his feet is empty of memories.[30]

This poem, dating from 1853, is strikingly reminiscent of the lyrics of Michel Rivard's 1970's song "La complainte du phoque en Alaska" (The Lament of the Alaskan Seal), where a performing seal is lured away to the United States by fame and fortune, only to find that when she grows old the fickle foreigners lose interest in her. "It's never worth leaving those who one loves/ To go off and balance balls on your nose/ It makes the children laugh, but it doesn't last long/ And nobody cares about you when the children have grown up." This song is a modern anthem of Quebeckers, sung in a thousand bars from Chicoutimi to the winter haunts of Florida, a testimony to the powerful impulse first expressed by Crémazie.

Crémazie, like most writers of the day, made common cause with the Catholic Church. At first this was not difficult for an artist to do. Clerics like the Abbé Casgrain were worldly and sophisticated in their way. Casgrain, for example, was an early folklorist, publishing (in 1861) a book called *Légendes canadiennes*. He argued persuasively that Quebec's cultural survival would be more meaningful if writers kept alive the folk memories of the past.

Without meaning to, Casgrain placed writers in contact with a powerful mythic current that would eventually escape the Church's control and enrich Quebec literature down to the present day. Habitant folklore "with its extravagant tales of good spirits and demons and supernatural happenings... has given a strong vein of fantasy to French-Canadian writing," says critic George Woodcock[31]— a vein that is conspicuously absent in English-Canadian writing.

The overt use of legendary material finds its best expression in Philippe Aubert de Gaspé's 1863 novel, *Les anciens canadiens* (Canadians of Old), the most popular novel of nineteenth-century Quebec.

This is a sentimental romance about the Conquest, in which Jules d'Haberville, a young Canadien seigneur, finds himself on the opposite side of the battlefield from his boyhood friend, the Scotsman Archibald

Lochiell. They had been students in Quebec together, and Lochiell had once come to stay with Jules' family.

The description of the family's feasts, where "the master of the house would be accused of stinginess if at the end of the repast the tables were not as loaded with food as when the guests sat down"[32] is rich in the sort of lordly nostalgia whose closest equivalent in English-Canadian literature would be the Jalna novels.

But there is a signal difference. Anybody who lives in southern Ontario knows that nothing remotely like the Jalna estate or the Whiteoak family ever actually existed in that place. *Anciens canadiens*, on the other hand, has the dense texture of a remembered world. The mother who plays a practical joke on the guests, serving them real snow instead of eggs "à la neige"; the raising of the Maypole, the songs sung by the girls and the rowdy roundelays of the men, come from a known past.

So, too, do the outright supernatural passages of the novel. Jules' servant's father, for example, is supposed to have seen the woman called La Corriveau, who was locked up in a cage for having murdered all her husbands. This is a legend of which variants are still being collected in rural Quebec today; in de Gaspé's novel, the servant's father is pursued by the monstrous Corriveau, whose skull has no eyes; she chases him into a congregation of torch-bearing demons on the Île d'Orléans. "He saw that the flames were running along the shore, as if all the cursed goblins had come there by appointment to hold their Sabbath."[33]

This occurs early in the novel, and it foreshadows the attack of the British many years later, who put to the torch all the houses on the Île d'Orléans, including that of Jules' father. The officer forced to carry out the burning is Archibald Lochiell.

The novel's successful fusing of folklore with history created a template for a series of Walter-Scott-like romances which would be the most popular genre in Quebec for 50 years. Many of these would recall both the Conquest and the Rebellion of 1837, and they would deal perforce with a question which haunted Quebeckers every day: how should they feel about "les Anglais," with whom they had now lived side-by-side for nearly a century?

Les anciens canadiens demonstrates the problem. Archibald is an English speaker, but as a Scot he can rail against British imperialism and deliver a necessary warning: "Mistrust the English," he cries, "a nation which has all the tenacity of a bulldog. If the conquest of Canada be necessary to her, she will never lose sight of it: witness my unhappy country."[34]

At the same time, much as he did in real life (his family had intermarried extensively with the British élite), de Gaspé finds it is necessary to reconcile the wounds of the past. Reminding Archy that they are "brothers in affection, but enemies on the field of battle," Jules asks what his old friend will do once the fight is finished. "I love Canada," replies Archy, "and after a peaceful and laborious life, I should at least lay my head beneath the same soil as you, my brother Jules."[35]

A similar conflicted attempt to heal the wounds of history emerges in *Les Ribauds*, Ernest Choquette's 1898 novel dealing with the Rebellion of 1837. Ribaud's daughter Madeleine has fallen in love with Percival, a British officer, much to the humiliation of her father. He hides himself one day in the woods beside a road where Percival will pass on his way to court Madeleine. The old man has brought a rifle, but when he sees the young Englishman approaching on the road, he finds he cannot kill him.

The sentimental framework of historical romance is not strong enough for this tragic dilemma. However, a reader can glimpse the unexplored abyss at the end of *Les anciens canadiens:* Jules marries an Englishwoman, but his sister Blanche refuses flatly to marry Archibald. The two are deeply in love but, declares Blanche, there is "a chasm between us that I will never cross." The couple will remain friends, locked together in a sterile platonic relationship which will produce no children— an early representation of "biculturalism" from the French-Canadian viewpoint.

A truer description of the irremediable pain which underlies the "reconciliations" in these early novels had to wait another 100 years, for the acid pens of Hubert Aquin and Michel Tremblay. As we will see in the chapter on language, the key missing element is "recognition" by anglophones of French culture in Canada. Without that, no reconciliation is possible.

Les anciens canadiens is the last of what might be called the early and free-spirited novels. *Charles Guérin* (1853) is another. Set in 1831, its broad canvas satirizes everything from romantic novels to early naive efforts to undermine the British.

The author, Chauveau, sketches Charles' naive plan (which oddly foreshadows Mahatma Gandhi) to undermine the British by organizing a boycott of their manufactured textiles. His friend Voisin, trying to imagine Charles' mother dressing in home-made Quebec cloth, is reduced to tears of laughter. "Do you think a woman who wears velvet will put on the étoffe du pays? It's impossible in the superlative." Charles joins in the laughter. "You're right. It's impossible squared, cubed even!"

This kind of highly educated kibitzing, which wouldn't be out of place in a novel today, is worth prizing, because it soon disappeared from Quebec fiction. The reason is foreshadowed in the dark portrait of Wagnaer, the Englishman who schemes to take possession of the Guérin family farm. Wagnaer has understood that the riverside property has great potential for future industry, and he justifies his aggressiveness (which includes tricking Charles into signing misrepresented documents) on the Lockeian grounds that the person most capable of producing wealth has the moral right and imperative to do so.

"First I try to exploit people to their own profit," he says. "That seems fair to me, to do good to others in doing good for oneself. But when people are stupid and get in my way... well, too bad for them, I exploit them as I can, because one always has to exploit. Otherwise there would be no progress. It's the fundamental rule of commerce."[36]

In this, Wagnaer is describing how capitalism has adopted the messianic imperatives of Calvinist Protestantism. No society has the right to refuse it, because to do so is to refuse a sort of "salvation."

At the time that Chauveau was writing his novel, the stand-off between the values of the two societies was strained and fraught, but still manageable. Undemocratic means were used to prevent the French, still a majority in Canada, from frustrating the desires of the anglophone minority. The joint legislature set up in 1840, for example, provided Ontario with as many votes as Quebec, even though Ontario's population was smaller.

This kind of political injustice was the equivalent of business ethics as practised by Wagnaer. It was disagreeable, but hardly severe by mid-nineteenth-century standards. The French were realistic enough to appreciate this.

But the situation worsened. The Orange Order, the ethnic arm of Protestantism, had been fairly marginal in Canada until this time. "However, as the century progressed, the order moved closer to the centre of the political stage... in Toronto during the 1850's contempt of Catholics and French Canadians was elevated into a patriotic duty."[37]

By the end of the 1840's, through relentless immigration, the British government finally achieved its goal of making anglophones a majority in Canada. Quebec's surviving liberals understood that one man, one vote was a recipe for cultural extinction in a country where the majority was increasingly hostile. They could not effectively defend democracy under such conditions, although some continued to try.[38]

Meanwhile, the Catholic Church received reinforcements. The 1848 revolution in France had brought to power an anti-clerical regime, and the élite of the French Church fled to Canada, bringing with them the doctrine known as "ultramontanism," which held simply that every Catholic's first allegiance must be to the Pope, who (from a French point of view) lived "across the mountains"— "ultra montes."

For artists and writers, the Great Darkness (la Grande noirceur) began when the Catholic Church seized control of education in Quebec in 1875. The vacantly smiling, cult-like happiness of the Catholic villagers in the novel *Jean Rivard* would become general in Quebec literature. Any realistic discussion of human relationships, especially sexual ones, was taboo.

At the same time it became more acceptable to demonize the English. They, after all, were Protestants. Hence the dreary procession of romans du terroir which promoted the clerical vision of a servile agricultural paradise until Ringuet's *Trente Arpents* and Guevremont's *Le Survivant*—novels which bookend World War II.

This is also the period during which fascist ideas gained a certain currency among the clerical and intellectual élite in Quebec (as they did in Great Britain). But "popular support was relatively small" for writers who were attracted by these ideas."[39]

The real motivating force of Quebec fiction during this time was the longing for nationhood. "In this country the social question is the national question; there is no other one,"[40] wrote Pierre de Grandpré in his novel *La patience des justes* (The Patience of the Just). This echoes the thinking of Jean-Charles Falardeau, an influential sociologist turned literary critic, who argues that Quebec literature continues to embody a "political romanticism" even today, in spite of the fact that "the social tissue can no longer hold the individual in the axis of traditional relationships." Modern novelists with great differences of opinion still embody the ideology that "the French-Canadian nation must survive. The permanence of the collectivity as well as the permanence of a mission which it must fulfill are affirmed [in their books] with insistence."[41]

Secular writers like Roger Lemelin and Gabrielle Roy wanted self-determination for their province so that it could chart its own course in the modern world. The ultramontane Catholic authors who continued to be influential during this time also wanted self-determination for Quebec, but for a different reason: they wished to freeze its values in time.

Clearly there was no love lost between these two camps, but they did agree that their goals could not be attained so long as Quebec was part of Canada. They also made common cause in resisting the inroads of American consumer culture in Quebec. And finally, of course, even the most anti-clerical authors would rally to the defense of clerical authors who were attacked by English-Canadian critics. This partly accounts for the tendency until very recently in Quebec to defend the indefensible: the fiction of Lionel Groulx and Félix-Antoine Savard.

Those who wish to believe that Quebeckers during this time were, in Mason Wade's tongue-in-cheek expression, "fascist at heart, totalitarian, authoritarian"[42] need look no farther than Lionel Groulx' novel *L'Appel de la race* (1922) or Félix-Antoine Savard's *Menaud, Maître-Draveur* (1937) with its dithyrambic ecstasies of anti-English paranoia. Both of these authors were Catholic priests.

But those who look farther will soon discover that the Church had become the fist, not the heart, of Quebec. Quebeckers allowed it to do the tough fighting that was necessary during a time when racism in English Canada reached unprecedented levels. Consider, for example, that Groulx wrote *L'Appel de la race* in response to Ontario's Regulation 17, whose intention was to extinguish the large French minority in that province. Groulx' hero, Jules de Lantagnac, is an assimilated francophone living in Ottawa who is so outraged by the Regulation that he leads a crusade against it in Parliament. It is evident, I think, that without the Regulation's creator, Ontario premier Howard Ferguson ("an Orange bigot, narrow, fanatical, and anti-French"[43]) and others like him, there could not have been a Jules de Lantagnac— or a Lionel Groulx.

Menaud, Maître-Draveur (Menaud, River Boss) is perhaps the last, and the most anti-English, of these novels. It was inspired in part by the construction of an aluminum works by American Alcan in the Saguenay country. In 1928, Alcan raised the water level of Lake Kénogami to provide greater hydroelectric power. The farmers living near the lake had no recourse; they simply gathered what they could and fled.[44]

In Savard's novel, Menaud is an aging lumberman who finds that the common forest land of his village has been sold to an "English" company. His people, Durham-style, will have no future but to become employees of the company. To his disgust, however, only one man joins him in resisting the "outsiders." When Menaud understands that the battle is lost, he wanders into the forest and becomes insane.

For an English-speaking reader, this novel is very hard to take. It is not so much the attacks on the faceless English "usurpers," but the self-pitying contrast between them and the local people, confused by laws and monetary forces they don't understand, these "simple and sweet souls who tried to find their way, like travellers lost in a country obscured by mist and fog" and who "cried together like brothers born in the same cradle."[45]

By this time the majority of Quebeckers already lived in the city and were beyond the reach of Savard's rhetoric, which alternated between mawkishness and a starchy Catholic view of the land as a "sacred reliquary."

However, the novel has one quality which has given it an enduring place in Quebeckers' hearts, and that is the lyrical intensity of its description of the Quebec landscape. This is a territory of "quicksilver streams, the sapphire of blueberries, the perfumed canes of raspberries" where "in the new grass of shorn prairies crackle the vast choirs of crickets."[46] Again, everybody knew it wasn't so— the brutal, killing labour and winters of *Maria Chapdelaine* were much closer to the truth— but the *feeling* which it described was true. After 150 years of survivance, Quebeckers had become so tenderly and fiercely attached to their territory that even Johann Herder would have been impressed.

CHAPTER FOUR

Here is a ghetto   gotten for goyim
O with care denuded   of nigger and kike
No coonsmell rankles   reeks only cellarrot
Imperial hearts   heave in this haven
Cracks across windows   are welded with slogans
There'll always be an England   enhances geraniums
And V's for Victory   vanquish the house fly.
— Earle Birney, "Anglo-Saxon Street," Toronto, 1942

For all its beauty of language, *Menaud, Maître-Draveur* also illustrates that which is naive and untenable in the idea of a Herderian people— particularly since the Holocaust has intervened, an experience which destroyed two centuries of romantic optimism.

But if an organic society represents an unattainable utopia, so too does the opposite simplicity of the "atomized" and self-creating individual. Just as the ludic side of human nature is amused at the notion of a peaceable folk living in a valley and strumming guitars, the gregarious side understands that there can't be such a thing as an individual outside of the community. The truth is somewhere between the extremes, and the happiest— or luckiest— societies cluster there as well.

The resistance against the romantic extremism of ultramontane Catholicism was not long in coming in Quebec. As early as 1884, Félicité Angers published *Angéline de Montbrun*, an apparently anodyne story about a woman who struggles between worldly and spiritual love, finally choosing to take the veil. Recent feminist critics have demonstrated that Angéline in fact becomes deranged under the pressure to make the "right" decision, and that the book is an act of subterranean resistance.

Others soon followed. The clerical advocacy of folklore returned to haunt the Church in the form of Rodolphe Girard's *Marie Calumet* (1904), a novel inspired by a bawdy old song of the same name. Marie Calumet is a curé's housekeeper who can't seem to understand where the line is drawn between sacred and profane. In the novel's most famous scene she is unable to decide what to do with a bedpan used by a visiting bishop. It seems impious to empty it, so she seeks advice. "Monsieur le curé, what should I do with His Excellency's holy piss?"[1]

Even Octave Crémazie grew tired of simplistic patriotism. "Our country hasn't much taste in poetry. Rhyme *gloire* with *victoire* often enough, *aieux* with *glorieux*... heat together over a patriotic flame and serve hot."[2] By the turn of the century, novelists like Robert Lozé preached the benefits of getting technical training in the United States and setting up modern factories in Quebec, and not much later than that the satirical revue *Le Nigog* started attacking the Church— which, of course, reacted ferociously, but already with a tinge of autumnal resignation.

At the risk of stating the obvious, this social evolution was taking place *inside* Quebec. Crémazie's weary fatigue with "our country" had nothing to do with Canada. Psychically speaking, Canada had dropped off the French-Canadian map. So, at long last, had France. Quebec, for better or for worse, was a society evolving on its own. "We wanted a country, and to do that we had to create a heritage," writes Jacques Godbout. "Literature in Quebec became the fundamental aspect of a political discourse."[3]

This fact of autonomous cultural evolution is the determining difference between Quebec and English Canada. Psychologically speaking, most of the British and Loyalist settlers who by 1867 had only just finished clearing their land were quite happy to remain British citizens. The project to unite four colonies into a nation called "Canada" was little more than a gesture of economic self-defence against annexation by the United States.

Confederation was, by anybody's standards, a patch job of nation-making: we remembered to pick up an anthem, but absent-mindedly forgot a flag. And there was— something that English Canadians prefer to forget— no popular referendum. Both MacDonald and Cartier knew that the people of Quebec would have voted No. Instead, they browbeat Quebec's representatives into a narrow vote (27 to 22) in favour of Confederation. Most who voted for it did so out of fear of the United States. At least one, Antoine-Aimé Dorion, warned that if Confederation were voted "without the sanction of the people of this province [Quebec], the country will have more than one occasion to regret it."[4]

Culturally speaking, the ethnic British population of the three English-speaking provinces simply carried on as if Canada were still part of the United Kingdom. Lip service was paid to the governing romantic notion that a nation should have its own culture, and a Toronto-based artistic movement known as Canada First was duly put in place. But these writers, most of whom identified themselves as "imperialists," were attempting to square the circle. They were proud of their new country, but only insofar as it was part of the British Empire. Their emotional loyalty remained with the metropolis; only their bodies were in Canada.

Maybe that's why so much of their poetry compared Canada to an oversized athlete. Sir Charles G.D. Roberts, better remembered for his animal stories, wrote that Canada was a "Child of Nations, giant-limbed/ Who stand'st among the nations now/ Unheeded, unadored, unhymned."[5] Torrents of terrible verse by any number of writers described the rocks, the rivers, the twisted pines, the vaulting mountains. E.H. Dewart prescribed "a national literature" the way my mother prescribed cod liver oil, as "an essential element in the formation of a national character."[6]

It is hard to imagine that anybody much enjoyed this pompous, dutiful literature. It was, for one thing, lacking in human interest. There were few people in these empty landscapes, and certainly nothing resembling a nurturing human community. As Robert Haliburton sadly wrote, noticing the lack of excitement in the wake of Confederation, "Can the generous flame of national spirit be kindled and blaze in the icy bosom of the frozen north?"[7] (Perhaps not, but he did launch a deathless metaphor; a century later, Northrop Frye lamented that "the colonial position of Canada is a frostbite at the roots of the Canadian imagination.")[8]

Because their hearts were elsewhere, English Canadians simply reproduced English society, minutely and as dutifully as possible. There was very little spontaneity, joyfulness, or the shared commemorations of a growing community. Instead, there was a perpetual looking over one's shoulder. As Irving Massey has perceptively noted, in early English–Canadian literature, "community existed, and perhaps still exists, only in the form of readiness to answer the call of duty: indeed... for Canada, duty takes the place of nationality."[9]

In 1904, Sara Jeannette Duncan, a brilliant young journalist who became arguably the first serious novelist in English Canada, published *The Imperialist*, the story of a lawyer in fictional Elgin, a city much like Brantford, Ontario— her birthplace— who runs for Parliament on the platform that Canada's future lies in economic integration with England. "I see England down the future the heart of the Empire, the conscience of the world, and the Mecca of the race," declares Lorne Murchison.[10] His opponent, a free-trader, wishes to hasten the inevitable economic integration with the United States.

Elgin is a suffocating little city. Lorne's younger sister had "those qualities which appealed in Elgin... the quality of being able to suggest that she was quite as good as anybody, and the even more important quality of not being any better." Her family "had produced nothing abnormal, but they had to prove that they weren't going to."[11] Many years later, Alice Munro, born not too far from "Elgin," would write a short story called "Who Do You Think You Are?" which demonstrates that societies, once set in a direction, change little in several lifetimes.

The religion practised in Elgin is one of strict submission and joylessness, but no-one rises up against it. During a typical evening in the Murchison parlor, Lorne's elder sister holds forth: "A lot of our church people are going to stay at home election day," declared Abby. "They won't vote for Lorne, and they won't vote against imperialism, so they'll just sulk. Silly, I call it." Lorne's mother silences her by recalling the priorities: "Well, what I want to know is," said Mrs. Murchison, "whether you are coming to the church you were born and brought up in, Abby, or not, tonight?"[12]

One day, Lorne Murchison glances down a laneway at Elgin's farmers' market, overflowing with fat summer fruit and caustic farmwives bellowing at customers. He experiences a momentary hallucination. "At that moment his country came subjectively into his possession, great and helpless it came into his inheritance as it comes into the inheritance of every man who can take it, by deed of imagination and energy and love."[13]

But the vision passes. He shakes it off, like cobwebs, and goes on to make his final campaign speech. He mocks the Americans for having ruined half a continent with the "spirit of revolt." He compares America to "the daughter who left the old stock to be the light woman among nations, welcoming all comers, mingling her pure blood." Canada, loyal to the Empire, is no such slut.

When French Canadians looked at this society— and they didn't have to look any further than Westmount or the Eastern Townships— they shuddered and described it as "l'avant gout d'une nécropole" (a foretaste of the cemetery).[14] True, they had the Catholic Church to deal with; but no priest had ever— ever!— dared tell them not to laugh. "The house has been here a hundred years," says Jean-Marc in Michel Tremblay's play *La maison suspendue*. "My family had their fights here, they made up here, they screamed, stomped the floor, played the violin and accordion... memorable parties and crazy funerals. I'd have bought this house if it was falling down, just to keep the memories from fleeing up the chimney."[15] In English Canada, part of this recipe had been misplaced. "Ontario," says a character in Irish writer Hugh Leonard's play *Da*, "isn't that the place where there's a very great deal of outdoors and not very much indoors?"

Irving Massey, who grew up in Montreal's Yiddish area in the 1940's, notes in a recent study of Canadian literature that both the French and the Jewish in Montreal shared an "uproarious" community life. The English did not. "I cannot say that I understand fully why English Canada has not imagined itself in communitarian terms," he writes, adding that he has "not found, in most of the English-Canadian literature that I have read, satisfying images of social participation or 'stickiness' among people such as are rife in the novels of, for one, Michel Tremblay."[16]

Whatever this inhibition was, it was durable. The empty, inhuman landscapes of the Canada First movement are still present in the Canadian imagination. The vocabulary has changed— we no longer indulge in what Carl Berger calls the "crude environmentalism" of the early writers— but neither have we made ourselves at home in Canada. The last sustained effort to create a thematic vision of Canadian literature was Margaret Atwood's *Survival*, written in 1970. Although its language is up-to-date, it essentially repeated the grand old myth of a nation of lonely, atomized individuals hanging on by their virtuous fingernails in the teeth of an arctic gale.

About the only reference to French Canadians in *The Imperialist* comes from a grizzled party hack, who observes that whatever the merits of imperialism, it's a lost cause because of Quebec. The essayist E.K. Brown, writing in the 1940's, repeats this observation, adding that after the failure of the imperial dream, Canada "entered upon a period in which thinking was extremely confused."[17]

One can see the beginnings of this in Lorne Murchison's election speech. The noble verses inscribed on the Statue of Liberty, to him, mean little more than that the United States is lifting its skirts and "mingling her pure blood" with inferior races— a thought which Lorne rejects with a shudder of repressed eroticism.

Canada was, however, bound to adopt a similarly open policy. It was clear that there would never be enough ethnic British immigrants to populate the west. And yet if it were not populated by English speakers, the ever-fecund French might begin to fill the void. Worse, they were already there! They had settled the west in dribs and drabs for two centuries, in the process also creating the French-speaking Métis. In 1870, when Manitoba got its charter as a province, it was half French, and the Orange demagogues in Ontario were nearly hysterical with the need to get English farmers onto that prairie on the double quick. "The desire to see English farmers settle on the prairies presupposed that a new Canadian nationality [which was interpreted in racial terms by many] already existed as an ideal by 1900,"[18] an ideal proposed by, among others, Stephen Leacock, in his writings as an economist.

Since there were not enough English farmers for the vast west, the Canadian government reluctantly lifted its skirts to the Ukrainian peasants, followed by immigrants from equally remote locations. English settlers reacted to the presence of these groups by simply avoiding them. As prairie novelist Frederick Philip Grove— who himself had had to change his name because of anti-German prejudice— wrote in 1928, "The British will not mingle with [other immigrants]. Why not? From one single reason: from racial conceit."[19]

Sympathetic writers have argued that British Canadians were not inherently racist, but merely ethnocentric. They were proud of the accomplishments of the British Empire, and thought highly of themselves for being associated with it. What pushed them toward racial ideas were a number of "peculiarly North American anxieties"[20] created by the necessary presence of immigrant groups which often outnumbered them, and which needed to be anglicized. Nothing in their experience had prepared them for this task, and to say they were "confused" by it is putting it mildly.

This created an opportunity for racial theorists like the American Madison Grant, whose book *The Passing of the Great Race* (1916) lamented the "mongrelization" of America's English blood. He thought Canada could still avoid this fate and create "the finest and purest type of a Nordic community outside of Europe."[21]

Grant was popularizing ideas which had first been developed by the

Frenchman Arthur Gobineau. Gobineau had argued that there was a hierarchy of races, and that the superior ones were going to be tragically overwhelmed by the inferior ones. Gobineau certainly influenced a few French-Canadian writers like Lionel Groulx. But his ideas, through popularizers like Madison Grant, also arrived in English Canada and were widely spread by the poets and novelists of the young country.

There was one group which left these theorizers uneasy and very often flummoxed: the French Canadians. Just as they are virtually invisible in the world of *The Imperialist*— except as a gray and menacing block of hostile voters— so they remain largely invisible in English-Canadian fiction, from the beginning right down to the present day.

There may be a simple explanation for this: the French Canadian, if he is to appear in English-Canadian fiction, must perforce be speaking English. He may speak it badly, but he is already somewhat assimilated. In addition, he is physically *in* English Canada, far away from Quebec, whose internal life very few English-Canadian novelists have ever tried to portray. Where he is represented, it is as as part of the colourful ethnic background, a slightly moronic fellow with a funny accent. He joins the natives, the Ukrainians, and the Jews in the role of villain, sidekick or untrustworthy small merchant.

But in the end, those other minorities are assimilated and forgiven. The individual French Canadian may be assimilated, but he will never be forgiven, because his *group* cannot be assimilated. It is his group which killed the imperial dream, and that will not be the last of its crimes. Still to come are the conscription crises, the War Measures Act, and the independence referenda. "Johnny François," as he is described in *The Imperialist*, will wear his Gobineau colours long after the others have been welcomed into the Canadian family circle. He will always be part of what Madison Grant called "the indigestible mass of French Canadians."

Johnny François' fate was already clear by the time Charles Gordon wrote his first novel in 1902. Gordon, better known by his pen name

Ralph Connor, churned out extremely popular potboilers about the "virile Christianity" which would conquer the Canadian wilderness.

A recent book, *Racial Attitudes in English-Canadian Fiction*, analyzes the painful evolution of Gordon's attitudes toward natives, Jews— and French Canadians— in a series of bestselling novels starting with *The Sky Pilot*. From early stock stereotypes of Jews, Gordon gradually evolved over the next 30 years toward greater sensitivity. In his last novel, *The Gay Crusader* (1936), aware of what was happening in Germany, he tried, rather self-consciously, to create three-dimensional Jewish characters. Repenting his earlier narrowness, Gordon finally argued for "a new national unity that would wipe out forever from true Canadian hearts all the racial and religious jealousy and hate that has darkened the future of our Canadian life."[22]

However, Gordon was not able to accord his French-Canadian characters the same generosity that he found for other minority groups. In novels like *The Major, To Him That Hath*, and *The Runner*, French Canadians are shown to be either alcoholic, habitually lazy, or able to function socially only under the supervision of an anglophone. "Few other writers have depicted French Canadians so clearly as 'white niggers of America,'" concludes the author of *Racial Attitudes in English-Canadian Fiction*, alluding to the title of Pierre Vallière's 1968 book about the situation of francophones within Canada.[23]

Other writers who make allusion to the French in Canada also failed to imagine them as fully rounded human beings. Ronald Sutherland, who founded Canada's only faculty of comparative French and English literature at the University of Sherbrooke, made the following brief summation in 1971:

French Canadians can indeed be found in English-Canadian novels— there is Blacky Valois in Allister's *A Handful of Rice*, Gagnon in Callaghan's *The Loved and the Lost* and one of the prostitutes in his *Such*

Is My Beloved, René de Sevigny in Graham's *Earth and High Heaven*, Frenchy Turgeon in Garner's *Storm Below*... and a multitude of others; but these characters are generally either stereotyped or completely out of context.[24]

Until Hugh MacLennan wrote *Two Solitudes* in 1945, there wasn't a serious piece of English-Canadian fiction that put the conflict of French and English in Canada at centre stage. The omission is a curious one, because the period after the turn of the century was fraught with human drama. There was, particularly, the bloody-minded battle waged by Orange Ontario to drive the French out of the west. "It was in this period that the incredible and moving stories of the québécois diaspora outside Quebec emerged," writes sociologist John Conway, "stories of assimilation, ridicule, prejudice, and discrimination— even of training children to hide their French texts when the education inspectors came to town."[25]

The only acknowledgement of this struggle in the popular imagination of English Canada lies in the figure of Louis Riel, who is distant enough to have become the object of sentimental myth. He is the subject of books, films and even a 1967 opera by Harry Somers (in which, as an extra, I had the honour of hanging him). What is remarkable in these recountings, however, is how often the issue of the French language is marginalized, to be replaced by Riel the tragically misunderstood religious mystic. I remember once, as an arts reporter in the late 1970's, going on the set of an English-language TV movie about the Riel rebellion. The widow of Thomas Scott, the Orange agitator hanged by Riel's government, was portrayed as a doughty heroine. The Quebec actor who played Riel, Raymond Cloutier, explained to me during a break that he was having trouble getting the director to understand that Riel wasn't *entirely* just a picturesque lunatic.

As the hanged king of a French-Canadian west that never came to be, Riel has continued to inspire a certain delicious "obscure sentiment of guilt"[26] in writers like Margaret Atwood. But this literary activity serves to mask the conspicuous absence of attention to the everyday destruction of the French language which has continued in the west until the present day. Less than 10 years ago, for example, the people of Saskatchewan successfully pressured their legislature to refuse official status to French— even though the Supreme Court had ordered the province to respect its bilingual charter. Given current Canadian sensibilities to minorities, it is significant that such measures, when taken against francophones, stir little if any reaction.

Why was this ferocious ethno-linguistic war omitted from the imaginative record of English Canada? To some extent, as we have seen, the French were victims of a general rise in racist sentiment which occurred throughout North America at the end of the last century. But there was this difference: no other minority group was daring to claim a place for its *language* in Canada. This explains why, when the Canadian army defeated Riel at Batoche, it conducted a methodical campaign of burning Métis settlements with the purpose of driving French speakers out of the territory.[27]

The will to impose the English language on the west was nourished, as Christian Dufour argues, by the belief that the new territories were part of "the conqueror's inheritance."[28] Conversely, the will to forget the episode is part of a general embarrassment with this aspect of our national past. It accords poorly with our self-image as a kinder, gentler people.

These conflicting attitudes can be illustrated with reference to *Saturday Night* magazine. In 1890, Edmund Sheppard, the Toronto-based magazine's founder, slandered several Quebec army officers who had served in the campaign against Riel. He called them cowards. When Sheppard was sued in Montreal he simply refused to go, implying that it was beneath an Englishman's dignity to answer a subpoena from a French court. Sheppard unhesitatingly linked the western settlement issue to the Conquest. "Those of us who believe that the Battle of the Plains of Abraham was fought for something... will not permit the extension of French in the new territories."[29]

Two decades later this anger seems to have been sublimated into willed forgetfulness. "There is hardly one man in a hundred of the citizens of Ontario and the west who gives a thought to Quebec except at election time," reported *Saturday Night* in 1912.[30]

It is often assumed today that English-French tensions at the time were principally religious, and that language has only emerged as an issue in recent times as religion diminished in importance. But in fact there was lively debate at the turn of the century about the meaning and practicality of speaking two languages within the same country. The Equal Rights Movement argued that Canadians would not be equal until they all spoke the same language, and its leader, Dalton McCarthy, laid out the reasoning in a sophisticated presentation to Parliament on February 18, 1890.

Addressing an audience which included Wilfrid Laurier and Hector Langevin (after whom a block of the Parliament buildings is named), McCarthy stated that the French in Canada were "a bastard race" because non-English speakers could not fully participate in the life of the North American continent. He carefully explained that by "race" he meant any community united by a common language. He was aware, he emphasized, that the new science of anthropology had put an end to any notion of definable physical differences between races.

> A common language establishes a kind of intellectual fraternity which is a common link much stronger than that created by the real or supposed community of blood. We are strangers in each other's eyes if we have no common idiom... it is only through identity of language that men are grouped into nations.[31]

McCarthy argued, in effect, that there could be no true community between French and English in Canada until the French became invisible through assimilation. Once the French understood that everybody would be happier and more prosperous this way, he was sure they would agree. Above all, he declared, he was innocent of "any hostile sentiment to the

French-Canadian race."[32] He was, in Charles Taylor's terminology, a believer in "instrumental thinking." Excessive languages were like excessive decoration on a tool or a machine, a relic of old-fashioned thinking.

That day in Ottawa, Hector Langevin observed incredulously that "he wants to destroy our race from the Atlantic to the Pacific." But McCarthy was innocent of any awareness of the pain caused by wrenching away another human being's identity. He was serenely convinced that the French would be, as Jacques Godbout put it, "happier. Happy," once transformed into anglophones.

Whatever McCarthy's underlying motives might have been, his remarks about language were perceptive. Quoting Lord Durham, he asked how there can be national feeling in a country divided into two populations which cannot communicate their experiences to each other?

Ultimately, McCarthy and his allies were successful in the west. Three provinces passed unconstitutional laws (and Ontario the dubious Regulation 17) to outlaw French schools, thereby breaking the thread of the language in a couple of generations. But Quebec settled into a siege mentality, contenting itself with securing modest measures of linguistic recognition. By 1910, it was established that business within the Quebec government would be conducted in French. By the early 1930's the federal government was persuaded to put the words "deux" "cinq" and "dix" on the currency, alongside the words "two" "five" and "ten." To our eyes today the measures seem small indeed, but they were fiercely contested.

Unlike writers elsewhere in Canada, those of the anglophone community within Quebec might have had direct experience of the French population. But a rigid social structure had grown up which prevented the groups from knowing each other. Among the upper class, debutante balls such as that held by the St. Andrews Society ensured that marriageable young anglophone women were unlikely to encounter francophone suitors. Among working-class anglophones, sometimes forced to inhabit the same neighbourhoods as francophones, mutual disdain generally succeeded in separating the groups— a situation which was memorably dramatized in David Fennario's play *Balconville*. Claude and Johnny have been "friends" for a long time, but strictly in English. One day Claude loses his job, and Johnny's wife persuades him that it would show respect if he would express some sympathy... in French. The play's climactic moment is when Johnny, for the first time in his life, forces a few words of the hated language out of his mouth. "J'ai... de la peine... que t'as perdu... ta FUCKING JOB!" This is what the linguistic philosophers call "recognition." A little of it goes a long way: it is the beginning of authentic friendship between the men.

But *Balconville* is a work of our own time. In the post-war period, you'd have been likelier to see the ghosts of Wolfe and Montcalm kissing and making up under the Porte St.-Jean than such a work being written. During the first half of the century, anglophone writers in Montreal created a weirdly colonial literature in which life was carried on in a kind of tunnel connecting the English neighbourhood to the English church to the English offices downtown to the English bars where folks hung out after work. "Earlier writers like Stephen Leacock and Morley Callaghan," writes critic Michael Benazon, "very often wrote as if Montreal were a purely English-speaking city."[33] The two communities, in Mavis Gallant's phrase, were like "schools of tropical fish," each moving as a mass, and each possessing collective reflexes to avoid the other.

Once it occurred to Hugh MacLennan to write *Two Solitudes,* he must have felt as if he'd stumbled on a literary gold mine that everybody else had somehow overlooked. You can feel the excitement of exploring this terra incognita of the heart in the book's opening words: "Northwest of Montreal, through a valley always in sight of the low mountains of the Laurentian Shield, the Ottawa River flows out of Protestant Ontario and into Catholic Quebec. It comes down broad and ale-coloured and joins the Saint Lawrence, the two streams embrace the pan of Montreal Island, the Ottawa merges and loses itself..."[34]

The book recapitulates the differences between French and English

Canada as understood at the time of its publication in 1945. Athanase Tallard, a hereditary seigneur and federalist member of Parliament, keeps up the noble struggle for the recognition of his people within Canada. His separatist son Marius holds him in contempt, while his other son Paul— under the influence of Athanase' anglophone wife— tries to feel his way toward a fusion of his parents' cultures.

Athanase tries to prove that French Canadians can be good business-men, but is abandoned by his priest and community for his pains; and then by his anglophone business partner, to whom Athanase' only use was as a conduit to the French community. The old seigneur dies bankrupt and broken in spirit.

The second half of the novel traces his son Paul's romance with Heather Methuen, a daughter of Montreal's Anglo-Saxon ascendancy. She has broken free of the hidebound attitudes of her family, and she approaches Paul as an equal. MacLennan made it clear that their marriage was to symbolize the future of Canada, a harmonious blending of English and French.

Worldwide sales of MacLennan's novel hit 700,000 by 1967[35] and are probably over a million today, making it the imaginative work that has had by far the greatest influence on English Canada's understanding of French Canada. Clearly, the novel fulfilled a need, and in its time probably did a great deal to liberalize attitudes. It acknowledged the arrogance of the anglophone ascendancy in Quebec. It provided a positive role model of a sympathetic "Anglais" in the figure of Yardley, the old sea captain who has become bilingual and made friends with Athanase Tallard. The marriage of Heather and Paul, somewhat shocking by the standards of the time, offered hope that the awful strain of Canada's informal apartheid could be ended.

But to a bilingual observer today, such as translator Linda Leith, the book is implausible and actually perpetuated the attitudes it condemned. In a careful reading she shows that Yardley and Athanase always speak to each other in English, which upholds the old pattern that where both languages are available, English predominates. She also notices that francophone characters who stand for the self-affirmation of Quebec culture, such as Father Beaubien and Marius, are treated as "narrow-minded" or "racist."

> MacLennan is deeply suspicious of French-Canadian nationalism... without showing any awareness that his own Canadian nationalism exposes him to some of the same criticisms... [he] associates French-Canadian nationalism and particularly Marius' gifts as a demagogue with Nazism and Adolf Hitler.[36]

Most troubling is the character of Paul, who is represented as a francophone growing up in an entirely French village (although incidentally learning some English from his mother). Once placed in a boarding school in Montreal, Paul begins to think and function immediately as an anglophone. Later, when he decides that his vocation is to be a novelist, the writers that he mentions as influences are British or American. It is not so much that he has been assimilated, observes Leith, as that he was never— as an imaginative creation— French in the first place.

It is understandable that MacLennan and his original readers (circa 1945) might have overlooked the problem with Paul, which, once noticed, makes his "symbolic" marriage with Heather meaningless. This is not a portrait of an intercultural marriage. It is a mere anglophone fairytale, featuring a pretend francophone who poses none of the difficulties for Heather that a real francophone would.

What is more troubling to Leith is that anglophone critics during the next 45 years did not notice the problem. French critics did, but "the almost complete separateness of the French and English literary worlds of Canada"[37] prevented the message from getting through.

In 1967, MacLennan returned to this theme with *Return of the Sphinx*, widely considered to be a literary failure. But it also demonstrated how threadbare his character categories had become in the light of the Quiet

Revolution. He is still rhetorically sympathetic to French Canadians, but the separatist characters once again are presented as demagogues and terrorists. The anglophone hero, the politician Bulstrode, offers little more than Pierre Trudeau's doctrinaire liberalism as a cure-all for the situation.

Nonetheless, MacLennan paved the way for other writers trying to approach the subject. Some of these, such as Mavis Gallant, have acknowledged their debt to him. At the same time, as Quebec anglophone society gradually liberalized, it became possible for there to be anglophone writers also fluent in French. These— and here names like Clark Blaise and Mavis Gallant come to mind— were able to cross the language barrier and create more realistic francophone characters than MacLennan or his predecessors could.

Blaise, for example, worked with the fact that he had been brought from the United States to Quebec as a child, and thrust into a French community where he had to learn the language in order to survive the adolescent jungle. Mavis Gallant was sent to French schools as a child, even though her parents could not speak the language. Both writers are alert to the fact that anglophone Quebeckers *resisted* French because their status as a ruling élite depended on forcing the French to speak English. In Blaise' story "North," the young boy who recounts the tale remembers that his mother "was one of those western Canadians of profound good will... who could not utter a syllable of French without a painful contortion of head, neck, eyes and lips. She was convinced that the French language was a deliberate debauchery of logic."[38] In the Linnet Muir stories, Gallant also creates an autobiographical heroine, a brusque young pre-feminist who went to French schools but knows enough to keep the language to herself in the anglo milieu where she lives. She hears her father deliberately contort the French nanny's disapproving "pas si fort" into "passy four," the kind of insulting mispronunciation meant to remind the dominated who is in charge.

Both writers demonstrate, perhaps for the first time in English-Canadian literature, a respect and affection for French culture (as opposed to romanticizing it from afar). Gallant, for example, understands the communitarian "stickiness" which Irving Massey mentions as one of the defining differences between the two cultures. When Linnet Muir returns from New York, she does not go to live with her chilly family, but rather with Olivia, the nurse she has not seen for many years.

> Believing that I was dead, having paid for years of Masses for the repose of my heretic soul, almost the first thing she said to me was "Tu vis?" I understood "Tu es ici?" We straightened it out later... On her deathbed she told one of her daughters, the reliable one, to keep an eye on me forever.[39]

Even Linnet's imagination is affected by going to a French school. As a girl she ran one day into the traffic, believing Satan— "furry dark skin, claws, red eyes, the lot"— had appeared and urged her to do so. "I had no idea until then that my parents did not believe what I was taught in my convent school."[40]

Gallant wrote these stories in the mid-fifties. A little later, in 1967, Hugh Hood was able to go farther, writing stories about French Canadians, in English, in which no anglophone characters appear. A farmer sells his land to a mall developer; a stereo salesman falls in love with a girl on a bus; Gilles the garage mechanic is beaten by the police in an independence demonstration. In these everyday stories of Quebec as it existed 30 years ago, we have the impression of overhearing small dramas taking place in French to which we otherwise would have no access. Hood allows us finally to pull aside the curtain which prevented Bruce Hutchison from seeing the "exotic" life of Quebeckers.

Is it so exotic? Not in a large or melodramatic way. But the small touches and tonalities are certainly not those of English Canada. The policemen who beat up the demonstrators are unhappy to do so because they covertly admire disorder in a way that is, as the old writers would say, unthinkable to the Anglo-Saxon mind. And when Gilles, bleeding from several head wounds, by chance meets a young woman named Denise whom he has not seen for several years, she confronts him with the sang-froid of an intimate family member. "What's the matter with you, you're a mess." Informed he has been beaten by the police, she replies calmly that *she* has been "visiting the Archambaults," but she'll walk him home. En route she explains why young rioters are "fools, babies" and how the the student leaders of the movement make sure it's garage mechanics who get their heads split. She is 19 years old, and embodies an assertiveness arising from the old Quebec matriarchy that would be implausible, to say the least, in her counterparts in Toronto or Calgary.

A nation secure in its cultural identity, Charles Taylor has pointed out, is in a better position to be generous to a minority. But English Canada is not permitted to think of itself as a "nation," or to define a cultural identity for itself. So it is not surprising that English-Canadian writers are flummoxed as to what to do with Fench-Canadian characters.

At the present time, English Canada has not even succeeded in naming itself as a geographic entity. As political scientist Reg Whitaker has pointed out, the word "Canada" defines an entity which includes a place called Quebec. There is actually not a name for the rest of the country; nor is there likely to be.[41] The doctrine of national unity, as elaborated by Trudeau, forbids English Canada to develop its own identity; to do so would tend to accelerate the departure of Quebec.

A certain number of English-Canadian writers have made their peace with this situation. These are the words Robertson Davies puts in the mouth of Solly Bridgetower in *Leaven of Malice*: "Why do countries have to have literatures? Why does a country like Canada, so late upon the international scene, feel that it must rapidly acquire the trappings of older countries— music of its own, pictures of its own, books of its own— and why does it fuss and stew... when it does not have them?"[42]

One can't help remembering that Davies also was born not very far from Sara Jeannette Duncan's "Elgin"; it has always seemed to me that, with his morning suits and bright sideways glances, he was the last lovely exhalation of the imperial dream in Canada. But his airy dismissal of national literatures is hollow, because Davies himself was not above the need for a national identity. His nation was the England of literature and imagination, and having it, he needed no other.

But that is not a solution for the rest of us, as witness the far more frequent expressions of lostness that we hear from Canadian writers. Frederick Philip Grove, for instance, esteemed himself a failure because "I never had an audience: for no matter what or no matter who may say, he says it to somebody; and if there is nobody to hear, it remains as though it had never been said."[43]

Or Irving Layton: "A dull people,/But the rivers of this country/are wide and beautiful. A dull people/enamoured of childish games,/but food is easily come by/and plentiful... A dull people, without charm or ideas,/settling into the clean empty look/of a Mountie."[44]

Throughout most of Canada's history, the chief danger to the development of a national culture seemed to be the probing hegemony of America, wonderfully imagined by James Reaney as a fantasy of driverless automobiles wandering the highways. Thinkers about Canadian writing have generally assumed that literary and national boundaries should be, by some sort of act of God, in the same place. Northrop Frye knew better, but agreed that "culture seems to flourish best in national units (as opposed to Imperial or provincial poetry)."[45] This was also the belief of the cultural nationalists of the 1960's, whose testament was Margaret Atwood's thematic analysis of Canadian literature, *Survival*.

It is, however, undeniable that writers in both English and French Canada in the recent past have become so individual and idiosyncratic that thematic overviews seem no longer to function. Marie-Claire Blais' *Une Saison dans la vie d'Emmanuelle* is a satire of the *Maria Chapdelaine* tradition, and so in a way is part of it, but how to thematically link later works set, for example, in the lesbian club scene in Montreal?

Some critics, like Jacques Godbout, have apocalyptically predicted that traditional culture throughout the world— and in Quebec— will collapse under the impact of consumerism and a resulting art made of private concerns and literary navel-gazing. "The irritated consumer has replaced the citizen in revolt... liberté, égalité, fraternité have become: variety, publicity, satiety."[46]

Because this is a global situation, American penetration per se is no longer the central problem. It's as if the world were a ship whose cargo hold had previously been divided into compartments in order to ensure the vessel's stability. Suddenly, the walls of the compartments vanish and the contents mix, sloshing vaguely from fore to aft as the ship loses forward momentum and begins to wallow.

There are some who welcome this state of affairs, particularly anti-nationalist littérateurs such as critic John Metcalf. He argues that writers cannot be sealed off from outside influences, and that the only societies with a "tradition" are tribal societies.[47] This would certainly come as a surprise to authors like Aldous Huxley, who argued that it was only through their writers that "Frenchmen and Englishmen know exactly how they ought to behave." And it is difficult to imagine George Bernard Shaw's flights of wit, had he not had a clear idea in mind of the Englishman whose foibles inspired him, or Shakespeare's Henry V asking his soldiers to remember St. Crispin's Day, had Shakespeare not believed that an English identity had coalesced around the great events of its history.

Metcalf's argument is an old one, going back to the ancient question of whether the artist merely holds up a mirror to nature, or whether he or she creates models that inspire emulation.

In the past, the absence of consideration of French Canadians in English-Canadian literature was not an accidental thing. In my view, it reflected the existence of a national will, or at the very least of strong preferences widely shared by English Canadians. This was a "nation" negatively defined by its prejudices, and that is not a very good kind of nation; but at least it is something, which can grow into something better.

If, however, we now take the view that a writer's choice to deal or not to deal with French Canadians reflects nothing but that writer's personal preferences, then we are saying that our literature reflects nothing. I do not find this argument convincing. Robert Lecker, a teacher of Canadian literature, grants that these ideas can be argued intellectually, but must be rejected "emotionally... I want to find a Canadian community; I believe there are Canadian ideals." The anti-thematic "argument does little to come to terms with people's apparent desire to make connections between their experience of the past and the present." It is little more than "ideological narcissism that thrives on itself, rather than on any shared notion of community."[48]

As it happens, Lecker is a Trudeau federalist who believes that the community in question should include both English and French Canada. Clearly we disagree about this. But his observations on the need of any human community for a collective expression of its values are convincing.

This still leaves the question of whether Canada *has* in fact developed a genuine literary canon which expresses its nationhood. Because, in my view, there are two nations within Canada, the question has two answers. With regard to Quebec, very clearly, in spite of Jacques Godbout's anxieties, there continues to be a virtual unanimity among writers that, as Pierre de Grandpré expressed it, "the social question is the national question." There are many very good writers, from Michel Tremblay to Victor-Lévy Beaulieu to Yves Beauchemin whose characters wrestle profoundly with the issue of what it means to live in French in their corner of America.

In English Canada, however, the unanimity that was possible when the nation defined itself as a place incarnating British values has now vanished. With it has vanished the certainties, however wrong-headed, which informed the novels of Ralph Connor and his contemporaries.

Today a Canadian novel may consist of Nino Ricci meditating on his soul's continuing entanglement with memories of Italy, or of Rohinton Mistry recounting the struggle of a Zoroastrian clerk with the corruption of India's government. These writers will eventually have to come to grips with the place in which they are living, but what, I wonder, are the shared values and issues of English Canada which will inform their future work?

An English Canada which is no longer an extension of British glory is going to have to get on with the job of naming itself, if it wants to go on being a place.

CHAPTER FIVE

Grand port of navigations, multiply
The lexicons uncargo'd at your quays
Sonnant though strange to me; but chiefest, I,
Auditor of your music, cherish the
Joined double-melodied vocabulaire
Where English vocable and roll Ecossic
Mollified by the parle of French
Bilinguefact your air!
— A.M. Klein, "Montreal"

At the same time that Hugh Hood was writing his *Around the Mountain* stories, Leonard Cohen described an independence rally in *Beautiful Losers* (1966):

> Many of the demonstrators wore sweatshirts inscribed with Québec Libre. I noticed that everyone had a hard-on, including the women. From the base of a monument, a well-known young film maker addressed the cheering assembly.
>
> — History! the young man called over our heads. What have we to do with History?
>
> The question inflamed them.
>
> — History! they shouted. Give us back our History! The English have stolen our History!

As the crowd's passions mount, the narrator feels "a hand slip down the back of my baggy trousers, a female hand...— Fuck the English! I shouted unexpectedly."

In one of Cohen's unmatchable tours de force, he and the anonymous woman behind him approach a climax as the speaker rants about "blood" and "shame." But the speech ends, as it were, before they do. The narrator cries out, "But you can't leave! I haven't come yet!"[1]

The passage is funny and the reader doesn't immediately notice the fear and anger behind it. The French may think that their history has been stolen, but to the anglophone narrator it is just a question of out-of-control francophones having a collective wanking session.

Where does Cohen's anxiety come from?

His book coincided with the sudden rise in Quebec nationalism and Québécois self-confidence that came with the Quiet Revolution. Like other English-speaking Canadians, Quebec's Jewish community had no use for separatism and joined the battle against it.

But where English Canadians generally are associated with the old overlord status of the conqueror, the Jewish community in Quebec can fairly describe itself as descended from refugees and survivors. Opposition to French nationalism by Jewish writers often takes the form of implying that the old corporatist anti-semitism of the Catholic church is alive and well, and that Jews would not be safe in an independent Quebec.

This is a potent political tool, and English Canada has welcomed it with open arms. Readers who laughed at the political demonstration described in *Beautiful Losers* were more than happy, 30 years later, to purchase Mordecai Richler's anti-French diatribe, *Oh Canada! Oh Quebec!* Even self-flagellating books on the subject by French Canadians, such as Esther Delisle's quickly translated *The Traitor and the Jew*, have sold snappily in the mini-ice-age of anti-Quebec feelings that set in with the independence referenda.

This is not a savory phenomenon. Anybody who has the least familiarity with anti-semitism in English Canada would find anglo concern for the Jewish minority in Quebec to be suspect, to say the least. But considering how restless Quebec has been since 1990, it is easy to see how books like Richler's are useful for intimidating the province psychologically. In this, English Canada is not much different from other countries which instinctively fall back on this kind of technique when minorities become difficult. The basic process here has to do with convincing the minority that it is not competent to rule itself. This usually begins with assertions of economic incompetence. If that fails, the minority quickly finds itself accused of something more debilitating: moral incompetence. One sets out to convince them that they have not yet learned civilized behaviour. As Lise Noel expresses it in her global study of intolerance, "to justify his radical control of his victims, the dominator must be able to accuse them of an absolute crime."[2]

If French Canadians are guilty of anything, it is of an understandable xenophobia which comes of two centuries of trying to hold their own inside an unsympathetic English-speaking country. But xenophobia, which is defensive behaviour, is not racism. Study after study has confirmed that racist groups in Quebec are as marginal as they are elsewhere in Canada.

The recent hysteria about supposed racism in Quebec has obscured the much more complex and interesting story of how the French and Jewish communities have related to each other in Quebec. Even a casual visitor to Montreal can hardly help but notice that traditional Jewish culture, from the all-night brick-oven bagel bakeries on Şt. Viateur to the eternal perambulations of the Hassidim on Hutchison Avenue, is much more alive in that city than anywhere else in North America, with the possible exception of New York City.

As we have seen, it has long been part of the rhetoric of English Canada to intimidate Quebec with the accusation that its nationalism is racist. As Mason Wade observed, the greatest excesses of this rhetoric occur when francophone nationalism is on the rise. When it declines, so does the rhetoric.

There has been a gigantic upwelling of French-Canadian nationalism since the failure of the Meech Lake Accord, climaxing with the 1995 referendum. It is not surprising, then, to see a re-appearance of the kind of rhetoric that equates Quebec nationalism with the Nazis.

What is different, this time, is that one of Canada's best-loved novelists has made himself the spokesman for this rhetoric. In doing so, Mordecai Richler has legitimized a discourse of contempt for French Canadians which takes us back to the darkest days of the last century, attempting to sweep away Hugh MacLennan's tolerance as if it had never existed.

The Jewish minority in Quebec has never been a large one— it was only about 110,000 people in 1971— but it has come to play a particular role in the imaginative battle that is being fought between French and English Canada. Its writers have, historically, written in English, and most of the serious ones have dealt with the anti-semitism which was so visible in Quebec in the years before World War II.

But within this community of writers, two tendencies are evident. One, of which we tend to be aware in English Canada, involves people like Richler and Cohen, who have adopted a closed and mistrustful attitude toward French Canadians. Often, the audience to which they wish to send this message is us, fellow Canadians outside of Quebec.

Another group, of which poet Abraham Klein is an example, has tried to enter into an imaginative relationship with the French community. Even though anglophone, these writers have tried to "bilinguefact the air," to express their willingness to suspend judgement and to invite French Canadians into a dialogue.

Klein was one of the important poets thrown up by the literary renaissance in Montreal's Jewish community during the 1930's and 1940's. He lived in the French-speaking east end, and learned enough French to take a law degree at the Université de Montréal.

This was, however, also the great era of Quebec anti-semitism, upheld by the corporatist clergy led by Lionel Groulx, and supported by the newspaper *Le Devoir*. For that reason Klein also wrote devastating poems addressed to bigots, including this celebrated passage in "Political Meeting": "The whole street wears one face,/ Shadowed and grim; and in the darkness rises/The body odour of race."[3]

Since Klein was also fond of the French language and the general atmosphere of Montreal, he evidently knew that most French Canadians were not anti-Semites. This is an act of faith and good will that has been performed by many Jewish artists, scholars and writers in Quebec over the years. Some of them, like Ben-Z. Shek, have become notable students of Quebec literature. Others, like Naim Kattan, became prominent journalists; indeed, Kattan helped to break the anti-semitism at *Le Devoir*, and for many years was a regular columnist there.

David Rome, an archivist of Jewish history in Quebec, has noted that Jews in Montreal kept the customs and flavour of their European communities much longer than was the case elsewhere in North America. In his view, this is because the many rural French Canadians who immigrated to Montreal between the wars themselves looked like an exotic ethnic group. "The presence of French Canadians (in the anglo-dominated Montreal of the period) opened up the possibility of recognizing other second cultures. In Montreal you never had to hide being different. The concept of being a foreigner never existed in Montreal. You were not a funny person with horns if you were caught reading the *Keneder Adler* [a Yiddish newspaper] on the bus. Jewish writers were comfortable from the beginning in this environment."[4]

Most were, at any rate. Some, however, refused to learn French and wrote in English— much like the Morley Callaghans and Stephen Leacocks— as if there were no French people in Montreal. One of these was Mordecai Richler.

In his appreciation of Richler's novel *The Apprenticeship of Duddy Kravitz*, George Woodcock hesitates over the character of Yvette, Duddy's girlfriend. She is the only significant francophone in Richler's imaginative output.

> Yvette, the personification of basic human decency, never really comes alive either as a character or a humour, partly... because he never gives her the speech that fits her background... Even as a Québécoise she is unconvincing, for her English is not that of a working-class French-Ca-

nadian girl but of an anglophone member of the Montreal lower-middle classes in the 1950's. There is a strange kind of indifference in her portrayal..."[5]

In failing to *observe* French Canadians, Richler was unconsciously adopting the ruling-class prerogatives of anglophone Montreal at the time. As Woodcock observed in another context, Richler suffers from nostalgia for the Montreal of his youth, which was also the Montreal of English-speaking ascendancy. Twenty-five years ago, before his views hardened into their present rigidity, Richler acknowledged "that the real trouble was that there was no dialogue between us and the French Canadians, each elbowing the other, striving for WASP acceptance. We fought the French Canadians stereotype for stereotype."[6]

Historically, it was almost inevitable that Jews in Quebec would become anglophones. Under the Bourbon ban on non-Catholic immigration to New France, Jews were excluded along with Protestants. Until the middle of this century they were barred from the French educational system, which accepted only Catholics. And of course, like most immigrants, Jews reasonably decided to assimilate to the linguistic group which controlled the economy and the jobs.

By the early twentieth century there was a large English-speaking Jewish community which carried on its internal cultural life largely in Yiddish. When the poet Yakov Segal arrived in Montreal in 1911 there was already Yiddish-language theatre being performed in Montreal's Monument National— built, ironically enough, by the St.-Jean-Baptiste Society as a home for French-Canadian nationalist art. Almost everybody's home was a salon for itinerant and often-hungry poets and would-be writers, as Irving Massey's description of his mother's apartment in the 1930's makes evident:

The wainscotting in the long, windowless hall was muddy olive; it was made of a nubbly oilcloth that gleamed slightly in the gloom. When those who had walked to the end of the hall and emerged into the living room, all of them— even Mr. Summers, who lurched (and who at one point may have sought an inappropriate familiarity with my mother)— when they came out at the end of the hall, all of them began to "babble of green fields," in Shakespeare's phrase... The great creation of that period was people, not literature. Some of the literature may have been great, but what stands out... is people. Everyone counted; everyone mattered. And everyone wrote, too. Their presence was what counted. Perel sometimes ate knobl [garlic]. Segal wore a long coat and liked chicken— leberlach. The people came and went in our house, constantly. Were the people the real works of art?[7]

Massey says that the communal life was so intense that "one lived one's private life as an outrigger to one's public life," with the odd result that one felt very satisfied as an individual. He feels the Yiddish community may have approximated Schleiermacher's notion of individuality *as* affective immersion in community. (Schleiermacher was one of those romantic nationalist philosophers of whom Elie Kedourie is so suspicious.)

Massey recalls a shockingly casual anti-Semitic incident from his childhood. He had a habit of catching fish from a rubber raft at a certain spot near Mont-Rolland, where his family summered. A rowboat full of French-Canadian kids pulled across his path and one of them said, in French, "You're always here on the river catching the fish— damned Jew." To this day, says Massey, he recalls "the hard, pointed tone of the young man."

Massey never forgot the anti-semitism, but he also noticed the similarity between the tight clannishness of the Jewish community and that of the French-Canadian community. He learned joual, but today only speaks it with his family(!), preferring a more formal French with French Canadians. A knotted relationship, but a relationship nonetheless.

In his book, Massey compares the communitarian literature of Michel

Tremblay to Sir Charles G.D. Roberts' lonely wilderness, and finds each emblematic of its culture. For all the anti-semitism Massey knew as a child, he easily prefers French Canada which "embattled though it may be, has a tradition, and a tradition is a society: English Canada, to some eyes, seems to have neither..."[8]

The difference between the outlooks of Massey and Richler is evident. Richler sees French-Jewish conflict arising from the two groups trying to please the angolphone masters. Massey sees the conflict arising from their trying to establish an organic community life in the same space. Where Richler sees them having nothing in common, Massey sees similar cultures. His view implies an eventual rapprochement, and it is not surprising that he himself became bilingual.

Ben-Z. Shek has traced the characterization of Jews in Quebec novels. From *Charles Guérin* in 1853 to Roland Legault's *Risques d'hommes* in 1950, the shifty, hooknosed merchant was the standard caricature. But *Le Survenant* (1947), which is often noted because its hero, a mysterious Stranger who inspires a moribund community to new life and turns out to be an anglophone, also contains a sympathetic portrait of a Jewish peddler. Gabrielle Roy's early novels were resolutely anti-Nazi, and the title character in *Alexandre Chenevert* is specifically a fighter against racism.

At this time, during the 1940's, French-Canadian writers were doing what Canadian writers like Charles Gordon had done during the 1930's: coming to terms with anti-semitism. Claire Martin, who wrote the first Quebec novel portraying the evolution of an anti-Semite into a tolerant human being (*Quand j'aurai payé ton visage,* 1962), admitted that she also had been anti-Semitic as a young woman. "It's not an easy thing to confess, since racism is the ugliest defect of mankind."[9]

As Naim Kattan observes, French Canadians had noted the many similarities between themselves and the Jews. Increasingly Jewish characters took on greater moral status in works of imagination, so that the gentle and pacifist Ethel in Claude Jasmin's *Ethel et le terroriste* (1964), persuades her FLQ boyfriend to give up violence. By this time, Jewish characters are often "masks behind which are concealed liberated and improved French Canadians," concludes Kattan.[10]

And of course, the young narrator in what is often considered the greatest Quebec novel, Réjean Ducharme's *L'Avalée des Avalés* (Swallowed by the Swallowed Ones), is Bérénice Einberg, who has a Catholic mother and a Jewish father. "At Mass," she says, "it's like in the synagogue: it's buttered with cinders and blood everywhere." Shek observes that Bérénice, obsessed with her pimpled face, is a symbol of a people who are colonized, who are continually told by somebody more powerful than they are, that they are *ugly*.[11]

It is distressing, but probably inevitable, that a certain number of Jewish writers unsympathetic to the French would volunteer as Gurkhas when it came time for the descendants of the old British imperialists to challenge Quebec nationalism.

Richler's *Oh Canada! Oh Quebec!* presents itself as an analysis of French-English relations, but it is almost entirely concerned with the supposed anti-semitism of the French. There is little attempt to generate a thesis or explain historical context. It piles up a series of anecdotes which portray Quebec's leaders as mendacious, and its popular culture as ridden with racism. Material demonstrating the contrary is omitted, leaving English-Canadian readers with a picture of Quebec that Ben-Z. Shek has characterized as "distorted and manipulative." In a typical passage, political writer Daniel Latouche is characterized as an anti-Semite because he once attributed a Groucho Marx joke to Woody Allen. Latouche, writes Richler, confuses "his Jewish comics, possibly because they all look alike to him."[12] The anecdote demonstrates some habits of thought employed by unilingual anglophones when they set out to wield the tar pot against French Canadians. It does not occur to Richler that Latouche, who is not a native speaker of English, might make errors of this sort because American culture is foreign to him.

Richler's book touches a particularly low point when it encapsulates the Patriote uprising in the following fashion: "One of the stated aims of the Patriotes' rebellion of 1837-38 was that all Jews in Upper and Lower Canada be strangled and all their goods confiscated."[13] Richler offers neither source nor context for this "monstrous accusation."[14] The only known source is a denunciation of the rebels to the British in 1837 by a certain Joseph Bourdon. David Rome has written that there is "no way of knowing" if it is to be taken seriously, or if it was just a "figment of fantasy."[15]

It is worth taking a look here at the role played by Jews in the Rebellion of 1837, a story little known in English Canada. It begins in the 1820's, when Louis-Joseph Papineau and the Patriote Party began to lobby in the legislature for Jewish suffrage. This was extraordinary for two reasons. First, Jews at the time were forbidden to vote anywhere in the British Empire. Second, Quebec had been a closed Catholic society since its founding, and there was certainly anti-Jewish sentiment among many Patriotes. But in the end the party rallied to the values of American liberalism, and began to call for the Jews' enfranchisement and religious freedom.

The British authorities were not pleased, but by 1831 the Patriotes had a majority in the legislature, and they duly passed a motion granting civil rights to the Jewish population. The governor refused to enact it, the Patriotes continued the pressure, and the following year the Privy Council in London acceded. The Jews of England did not get the vote until 27 years later.

That is why, when Papineau was pursued by the British army after the defeat of the rebels, he was able to seek shelter in the home of Ezekiel Hart, a Trois Rivières merchant and Patriote supporter.

Ben-Z. Shek, who has written extensively about nineteenth-century Quebec culture, had this to say about *Oh Canada! Oh Quebec!* in a critique which appeared in the Vancouver-based Jewish magazine, *Outlook*: "A close reading of Richler's book... shows it to be distorted and manipulative, determined as he is to paint Quebec's movement for self-determination in the most negative light possible."[16] Shek is particularly distressed by the book's egregious comparison of *Le Devoir* with the Nazi newspaper *Der Stürmer*, followed by chronologically vague allusions to *Le Devoir*'s supposed history of anti-semitism. In Shek's view, this invites the English-speaking reader to believe that *Le Devoir*, which has not published an anti-Semitic editorial for a half century, is still a racist newspaper today.[17]

Attacks of this sort on Quebeckers often exploit a difference between the French and English traditions of freedom of speech. The French tradition encourages people to say what they think, regardless of social disapproval, so long as they can defend the statement logically. English speakers, on the other hand, are taught to surround a contentious statement with a little thicket of moral qualifiers so that nobody can attack their motive for making it.

In my view, this is a measure of the lingering influence of Calvinism on English speakers. The French will never understand why anglophones turn a rational conversation into a procès d'intention (putting the speaker's intentions on trial). The English, for their part, will never shake off the Puritan injunction that prideful speech is proof of the devil's influence.

The gulf between the two approaches is evident in Gwethalyn Graham's 1944 novel *Earth and High Heaven*, where the character René de Sevigny discovers that his Scottish-Canadian father-in-law, while publicly friendly to Jews, is a closet anti-Semite. "At least," recounts the francophone with disgust, "we don't say one thing and do another."[18]

Because they didn't "hide it," French Canada of the 1930's left a wealth of rhetorical anti-Semitism. Today it is often cited by writers uninterested in the other half of the phenomenon: the striking lack of what Gary Caldwell calls "active anti-Semitism" of the window-breaking or job-denying variety.[19] The post-war disappearance of even the rhetorical variety indicates that genuine anti-Semitism was no more common in Quebec than elsewhere in Canada.

Today, some writers unfriendly to Quebec make use of this history to accuse the French of anti-Semitism. But it is not the only allegation that is used to belittle Quebeckers. Others accuse them of an irrational prejudice against anglophones; still others of a proclivity toward racism generally. All of these are instances of the phenomenon mentioned by Lise Noel, where a dominant majority seeks to undermine the confidence of the minority.

Not all writers engaged in this project, however, are members of the anglophone majority. There is also a scattering of francophones who have internalized an inferiority complex and believe that their fellows are guilty of what Ben-Z. Shek calls "exceptionalism"— that is, that the group to which they belong is exceptionally backward compared to the English-speaking majority.

An early example is Victor Teboul's 1977 book *Mythes et images du Juif au Québec*, which amassed negative comments about Jews from Quebec fiction and used them, without analysis or counterweighting examples, to indict francophones generally. This technique was employed more recently by Esther Delisle in *The Traitor and the Jew* (1993), which heaps up 200 pages of anti-Semitic excerpts from newspapers and academic journals for the 10-year period beginning in 1929. One can safely say, after reading it, that she has left no slur unquoted.

What is striking in her book, which began as a doctoral thesis, is the intensity of Delisle's rage— which is often directed against herself. She recounts, for example, how as a young student she had accepted the conventional wisdom: "I was still braying this foolishness."[20] The style is alternately self-hating and self-exalting. "If this research had the consequence of making sure that there would never again be a 'Traitor' or a 'Jew' in Quebec, it would give me a certain amount of satisfaction."[21]

The tone of this last sentence is remarkably similar to the messianic enthusiasm of William Johnson's condemnation of French Canada in *Anglophobie: Made in Quebec*. Johnson, like Delisle, is a bilingual French Canadian. His subject is not Quebec's anti-semitism, but rather its "anti-English-ism." He piles up 460 pages of quotations which aim, with an unevaluative single-mindedness very similar to that of Richler, Teboul and Delisle, to demonstrate that Quebec's literature is little more than an expression of bigotry.

Johnson, exalted by his labours, tells his readers, "I don't really seem to have written this book: it has written itself." Like Delisle, he acknowledges that the work may have weaknesses, "but I think my efforts have merited a response from Quebec's intellectual community... let us at last speak of this family secret. Let us cease hiding the skeleton of the Anglais in the closet."[22]

I think it must be fairly evident that this second category of discourse wants Quebeckers to understand not only that they are bigoted, but that they are *more* bigoted than other people.

Writers such as Pierre Anctil and Ben Shek assume implicitly that Quebec will find solutions to its own problems. Richler, Delisle and Johnson are most emphatic that Quebec is incompetent to do so. Quebec can find the road to the future only with the help of Canada. "Good God," cries Johnson, referring to the argument that Quebec must be independent in order to protect French, "shouldn't that be the best reason to call on the aid of a second government?"[23]

Richler, in the same spirit: "Without the rest of Canada acting as an increasingly bilingual buffer, [Quebec]... would revert to being a folkloric society. A place that people come from. Ireland without that country's genius."[24]

The profound message of these books is that Quebeckers are inferior— "Ireland without that country's genius." They can flourish only with the help and guidance of Canada. Reading these writers is a bit like reading a gigantic, especially lugubrious Ralph Connor novel (say, *The Major*) with little soldier Joe Gagneau going off AWOL and a wise Anglo-Saxon patiently reminding him that 'We'd all be in a pickle if everybody behaved like you, Joe.'

Anthropologist Eric Schwimmer describes this as the "cycle of tolerance" which is practised toward minorities within a nation. They may be accorded the political and economic rights of the majority, but "without ever being treated as true equals."[25] When they periodically become restive, the majority becomes intolerant toward them. When they back down, tolerance returns. What is missing is *recognition* that members of the minority are fully competent human beings. Such a recognition would break the cycle of dominance, and so it can never be accorded.

There is a problem introducing these subtleties to the discussion of Quebec anti-semitism in English Canada. In North America today there is a kind of puritanical horror regarding the subject of racism. Writers are determined to demonstrate their own purity, somewhat as writers of an earlier generation were determined to demonstrate that neither they nor the characters in their fiction were sexually degenerate.

A good example of this confusion arises in Terrence Craig's attempt to evaluate writers like A.M. Klein and Mordecai Richler. In his overall survey of racial attitudes in English-Canadian writing, almost nobody escapes suspicion. Since, in line with current notions, he is extremely wary of "ethnic" thinking, it is not surprising that he ends up feeling dubious even about notable anti-Semitic crusaders like Klein.

Klein is troublesome because he believes that Jews "must resist assimilation into a Canadian cultural whole that is worth less than Judaism is." It is also troubling that Klein supported Zionism, "a nationalist and possibly even self-consciously racial outgrowth of Judaism."[26]

In this same analysis, Mordecai Richler escapes censure because he represents the Jewish community as ethnocentric and creates characters who try to escape from it into a larger cosmopolitan world. He claims to be anti-nationalist. Craig accepts these claims at face value, overlooking the fact that Richler's novels are essentially a celebration of anglophone Quebec, while Klein's work is suffused with sympathetic images of French Canada.

Quebeckers themselves are less likely to be led astray. They are comfortable with A.M. Klein, who looked out of his ghetto and took pleasure in the "parle" of French; and they are uncomfortable with Mordecai Richler, who does not.

This is also the reason Quebeckers can understand somebody like Irving Massey, who thinks about racism by asking himself what it is that hurts *him*: what is its subjective aspect?[27] That is the beginning of a conversation.

In English-speaking countries today, subjective thinking about racism is not permitted. One is not allowed to contest the definition or to define one's own experience of it. "You don't understand your own victimization; we'll help you." "You're not aware of your racism; take a course."

Writers who hold that French Canadians are irremediably defective would— in normal times— merely be expressing a point of view. Other voices would rise up to question or criticize them.

But in English Canada, because of our profound identity crisis, and because of the narrow orthodoxy that has grown up around racism, little healthy discussion of the books of Esther Delisle and Mordecai Richler takes place. Instead, these texts are presented as a kind of revealed truth about Quebeckers. They become weapons, stockpiled for the forthcoming battle.

CHAPTER SIX

Pierre Gagnon-Connally catches me
with an invisible lasso
inserts in my mouth an invisible bit
and jumps on my back...
then he starts to give me orders in English
I don't know English
but on that hot sunny day of July
every word which comes
from the mouth of Pierre Gagnon-Connally
is clearly understandable
— Larry Tremblay, *The Dragonfly of Chicoutimi*

In Francis Mankiewicz' 1981 film *Les beaux souvenirs* (Happy Memories),
Viviane, a young Québécoise, brings her anglophone lover to the family's
country house for the weekend. R.H. Thomson plays the anglophone,
and for some time he says absolutely nothing as the others chatter on in
French. Finally he opens his mouth, and speaks— in English.

Thomson's character is perfectly aware that he is in Quebec. So you
might expect him to speak slowly and simply. None of it: he natters on
at full colloquial steam. In one scene he stops at a wreckers' yard; his
monologue sounds something like: "Yeh, needa new gas tank. Old one's
clapped out. Doesn't have to be the same model, jus' somethin' small 'nuff
t'stick in the trunka the car. Godennything like that?"

The wrecker, and Viviane's sister Marie, erupt into laughter. "Est-ce
que tu le comprends? (Do you understand him?)" asks the wrecker. "Pas
un mot (Not a word)," she replies, tears of hilarity running down her
face. Thomson's character looks on amiably, then wanders off and picks
out a tank by himself.

The point isn't to illustrate the all-too-evident fact that the French and English languages are not on an equal footing in Canada. This scrawny young guy, as it happens, would be equally funny in Oaxaca or Palermo. The humour relies on his inability to grasp the fact that he is in a place where *people don't speak his language.* In today's world, only an English speaker can behave this way.

Once immersed in a linguistic milieu other than that of English, one discovers how extremely common is the kind of experience depicted in *Les beaux souvenirs*. During a routine interview with Marie Malavoy, briefly the Quebec culture minister, an anecdote emerged concerning a recent visit to her parents' village in rural France. A Canadian hitchhiker had gotten off the beaten track and was trying to obtain directions back to the highway— in English. Malavoy watched him plod from one shop to the next, and from one person to another in the street, before she took pity and helped him out. "He would have asked everybody in the village, quite unsuccessfully, because clearly he had never been taught that there are places in the world where *no-one* speaks English."

The presumption that the English language has a special status in the world today is not a peculiarity of Canadians; it is an attitude shared by anglophones everywhere. In South Africa, where English-speaking whites are a minority even compared to Afrikaans-speaking whites— not to mention Bantu- or Xhosa-speaking blacks— one can find an astonishing presumption that English will be the future official language of the country. Afrikaaner playwright Albie Sachs recently recorded his frustration in trying to discuss this matter with English speakers. In doing so, he perceptively describes an attitude which often escapes description:

> Experience shows us that when you want to speak to anglophones about the language question, you encounter great difficulty. For most anglo-phones English is not a language at all, but rather the very air they breathe, and all these other things are languages. The language question,

for them, therefore consists of deciding what to do about all these other things.[1]

A final level of difficulty arises for anglophones living in North America. It is a rare thing in human history for a language to monopolize a continental land mass. A North American certainly meets immigrants with an uncertain command of English, but he knows very well that within several years those people will have become fluent. His conviction that English is the air breathed by everyone is not profoundly troubled.

Compare this situation with the far more common experience of a German or Spaniard coming across a Frenchman or a Greek within their national space. They will expect the person to make themselves understood, but there is no question of linguistic assimilation. Psychologically, the foreigner's homeland is always just over the horizon.

In North America the opportunity to create a continent-wide language monoculture was greeted with excitement in the last century. It was predicted (correctly) that this would help create an economic engine the likes of which had not been seen before. But even then a few sensitive souls, such as Lord Dufferin, expressed anxiety at the cultural implications. Dufferin went so far as to wish for the survival of French in Canada "as a happy variety in the midst of the monotony of one language, and a single set of customs and manners across an immense extent of territory."[2]

Far more typical, however— as we have seen with Dalton McCarthy— was the idea that tolerating another language in North America was the equivalent of failing to replace a grinding gear in a well-tuned machine. Not many people could have articulated their resentment of French in such terms, but certainly most anglophones soon became accustomed to living on a continent where they could expect immediately to understand anybody they met. Their own language, as a subject of reflection and thought, simply disappeared; it became "the very air they breathe," in Sachs' expression. Even today it is hard for anglophones to understand that speakers of other languages *do* think about language. "Since English is virtually the world hegemonic language today, it is difficult for those who speak it even to understand what it could be like to live under linguistic threat."[3]

On this particular subject, it's not surprising that French Canadians are probably among the most articulate human beings on the planet. By the late nineteenth century, books were being published on the problem of anglicisms (English words and phrases penetrating the French language). Some writers investigated the dialects of northern France to demonstrate that the joual spoken in Quebec was a legitimate form of French. In 1881 Oscar Dunn (francophone, in spite of the name) published his *Glossaire franco-canadien*, the first French-Canadian dictionary. He was also among the first to understand that the American model of individual rights was useless in protecting a minority language. "Liberty, let us recognize, does not suffice to resist the influence of that which surrounds us, unless we have exceptional motivation to keep our social autonomy."[4]

In the summer of 1971 I returned to Canada after a pleasantly squandered year wandering around Europe and North Africa. Among other things, I had picked up a serviceable command of French while living some months in Algeria and pretending to teach English in a technical school.

My principal interlocutors were Pierre and Christian, Belgian science teachers taking advantage of the elevated salaries available at the time to francophone professionals willing to live in post-revolutionary Algeria. Pierre had bribed a socialist official into letting the three of us occupy one of the "decadent" Mediterranean villas abandoned by fleeing French administrators during the revolution. After 15 years' abandonment, the villa was no longer especially decadent. We had to apply many layers of whitewash to the walls, inside and out; this is where I learned to use the word "couche" in its sense of a coat of paint. (Recent life experience in Quebec has taught me that it is also the word for diaper. This is a good example of what Lord Durham meant when he observed that each language has its own way of organizing reality conceptually. I often meditate on this over the change table).

Pierre was an especially hard teacher. He over-emphasized words as if speaking to an imbecile, and corrected frequently and ruthlessly. My ears burned a good deal of the time, and I began to understand how difficult it is to learn a foreign language when one already has an adult's ego. Had there been an anglophone quarter in the city of Oran, I might have fled; but there wasn't.

The solution was to push the adult ego out of the way and think of the experience in child-like terms as a protracted game. Otherwise, like Hugh Garner's character "Frenchy" Turgeon in *Storm Below*, I would have steadily reduced my speech to a simple "yes" or "no" in order to avoid humiliation. Instead, it was possible to push outward, forcing French to occupy the mental territory that had already been explored and settled by the English language. Success in using the subjunctive, for instance, seemed to deserve a small celebration. But Christian, the most phlegmatic of Flamands, was not impressed. Why would he notice the rare occasions when I *wasn't* getting it wrong? I began to associate him in my mind with the lemon tree (citronier) outside the kitchen window; that helped.

All of this took place two years after the passage of the Official Languages Act in 1969. Returning to Canada some months later I became, like most anglo-Canadians of my generation, an unquestioning admirer of Pierre Trudeau. It was easy to believe, in the heady atmosphere of sixties cultural nationalism, that Canada was about to climb to some as-yet-undefined sunny plateau of national achievement. That this should involve a fusion of the two cultures, and the embrace of the two languages, seemed entirely natural.

It was difficult to overlook, however, that my own tentative bilingualism was received differently in Toronto than it had been in Paris or London several months earlier. Many Europeans seemed to have a rough-and-tumble grasp of two or more languages, and made very little ado about it. They understood that language was a tool to use, not an acquisition to show off.

In Toronto, in spite of what is now recalled as an era of "openness" to Quebec, my speaking French caused discomfort. People pleaded the third-year university course they hadn't taken, or how they'd always meant to get around to it, or how pleasant it must be to speak a foreign language. I noticed they very rarely said anything *in* French. Within several months I became silent on the subject, and remained so until moving to Quebec 20 years later. That's when I came across this remark by the writer Solange Chaput-Rolland: "I've had enough of those eternal English-only conversations about the advantages of bilingualism!"[5] All of this, it seems fairly clear, is an expression of the linguistic monoculture that is fundamental in North America.

It wasn't evident in 1971, but with the Official Languages Act Pierre Trudeau had injected a massive dose of intellectual nonsense deep into the Canadian psyche. His motives were admirable— he wanted to save Quebec from a centuries-old survival reflex which risked cutting it off from the world— and his point of reference— himself— seemed to provide an answer. In short, if Pierre Trudeau could become flawlessly bilingual, why couldn't everybody else?

A few months ago I was watching one of those concrete cutting-and-coring trucks drilling a hole through a stone wall. The drill bit howled, and a hose blasted cold water into the sizzling excavation. There would, eventually, be a passageway through the granite. In somewhat the same sense, I wearily assured myself, new passageways for the French language would eventually criss-cross the folds of my middle-aged brain. But— oh— the drilling!

Most linguists now agree that children are born with an innate capacity for language acquisition. For reasons which make very good sense to the mechanism of evolution, but which otherwise appear somewhat macabre, this ability starts to shut down after the age of five. By the time a child reaches adolescence, language has to be learned consciously, by rote, and it is almost impossible to achieve complete (what I like to call "transparent") fluency.

In Montreal there are a few people— mostly francophones— in my immediate circle who speak both languages transparently. Some of them, like Trudeau, had the good fortune to be born into an intercultural marriage and learn one language from each parent. Others were sent to English school at any early age. One or two claim to have learned the other language in Montreal's laneways from playmates.

I don't want this to seem too cut-and-dried. It *is* possible for a hard-working adult to achieve an impressive degree of fluency. But it seems only to be possible for highly motivated people who are willing to change their lives. At the very least, you must be prepared to make friends across the linguistic divide, and to carry on these friendships in the other person's language. This means being at a disadvantage for a number of years, and negotiating the awkward fact that so long as you have a foot in both cultural worlds, some of your friends will be unable to talk to the others.

Undergoing this adventure, or tribulation, in one's own life helps in an understanding of the task Canada has set itself by attempting to be a bilingual nation. Certain basic realities become apparent. One of them is that between any two parties speaking different languages, it is only necessary for one to leap the gap. Which will it be?

In a one-on-one situation, the decision can be negotiated. In an intercultural marriage, it usually comes down to where the couple lives. Being in Chicoutimi, or Moose Jaw, imposes a common-sense solution. It is often the same between friends. I could ask my neighbours in Outremont to speak to me in English— some of them are reasonably able to do so— but the neighbourhood is French, and it seems both respectful and somehow natural to want to integrate myself into the lives of my neighbours. One of these, a photographer at Canadian Press, speaks to me in transparent English when we work together professionally. But when I meet him on the street near our homes he speaks to me in French. This is harder for both of us, but it has an up side which we both quietly understand. It is one more tiny thread which binds me into the community life of the quartier.

These situations are graceful, and positive, because they are freely chosen. The same, unfortunately, cannot be said for the collective interaction of the two communities. As we have seen, this has functioned as an expression of political power. In the east and the west, historically rooted French communities were destroyed by illegal laws and informal prejudice. Surviving francophone minorities in the west continue to be assimilated at the rate of nearly 50 per cent per generation, and are now so small that they can't sustain the economic or institutional structure necessary to attract the young. They are spiralling toward extinction.

English Canadians aren't very aware of all this, but if you understand enough French to watch television news you will find that you have a ring-side seat for the slow death of the language across Canada. It's visible nearly every night, as Radio-Canada teams in Regina, Calgary, Winnipeg and Vancouver try to find local francophones for reaction to breaking news stories.

Statistics Canada indicates that these surviving western francophones have the greatest difficulty convincing their children to learn and to use the language. Even the current adult generation makes small errors, mistaking the genders of nouns and so on. Quebeckers watching them on TV do not need to listen to Preston Manning's snarly revisiting of Dalton McCarthy's ideas to see quite clearly what the future holds. To get a flavour of what it's like to be French outside Quebec, try this passage from a Gail Scott short story, where a francophone girl has forgotten to remove an incriminating political button before going out with a local cowboy she fancies:

His eye was fixed on the button on her left breast. Des ailes aux grenouilles, it said, over a small blue frog with butterfly wings. "You French?" asked a well-honed voice tightening like a lassoo...

"You French?" repeated the well-honed voice honed even higher.

"Non. No. Mais. Ispeakit." A nervous tick titillated the pit of her stomach. The cowboy's eye flinted like steel in the mirror. He shifted into pass and the charger rose above the deep ditch into dry fields flaring with the fluorescent yellow of rape.[6]

If native francophones are unable to maintain their language outside Quebec, what are the chances of native anglophones acquiring it? This brings us to the delicate subject of French immersion education, which currently attracts over a quarter-million English-Canadian students each year.

French immersion is also a legacy of the Official Languages Act, probably the most successful surviving policy of the Trudeau era. It has been buoyed up by the idealism of English Canadians, and it is a credit to Canadians that the rate of enrolment in these courses has not diminished in recent years in spite of the rising Meech-Lake-driven frostiness toward Quebec.

It is easy to enumerate, if not actually measure, the benefits of immersion. It's not a small thing, for example, that a good number of enthusiastic québécois teachers have been sprinkled across the small towns of English Canada where they perhaps can help do something about the attitude problem of the cowboy described above. It's a good thing that a strong minority of English Canadians who are just now climbing the career ladder have got a serious grasp of the country's other language. This will certainly help French Canadians to feel that they are "recognized" by the majority, since immersion students "are speakers of a prestigious, majority language" who have agreed to learn the minority's language.[7]

But it should be kept in mind that only about seven per cent of students in English Canada are in immersion.[8] Parents who choose it say they do so to give their children better job opportunities and verbal skills, not to help the country; this suggests that immersion would vanish like the winter snow if a future Reform government, for example, put an end to the bilingualism requirement in the civil service.

And finally, immersion is most often chosen by well-educated, middle-class families who would likely have been part of Canada's thin layer of tolerant liberals in any event.

The relatively small numbers affected explain why these programs can claim success in places like Saskatchewan, where the vast majority of voters continues to refuse official status to the French language. And surely there is something quixotic about a province like Alberta, where the graduates of French immersion number over 100,000 and are growing, while the province's native francophone population numbers fewer than 60,000 and is shrinking.

The Official Languages Act was an attempt by Pierre Trudeau to realize Henri Bourassa's old dream of a Canada in which French Canadians could feel at home from coast to coast. It might have succeeded if it had been attempted in Bourassa's time— before the World War I— but it is by now very late in Canada's day.

There is no question that Trudeau's policies liberated a certain amount of idealism and goodwill among English Canadians. But they also created a great deal of wishful thinking, and at a stroke obliterated the common-sense vocabulary in which people used to carry on the conversation about the language dilemma in this country.

Consider, for example, Arthur Lower's observation about bilingualism. In his view, it went against the grain of human nature to learn a foreign language if there was no occasion to live in the region where it is spoken. For that reason, he argued, "only a very small portion of English Canadians shall ever have occasion to become fluent in the French language."[9]

This attitude was fairly common in the pre-Trudeau English-Canadian intelligentsia. In an unpublished survey of 61 anthologies of Canadian literature published between 1922 and 1990, McGill graduate student Cynthia Sugars looked at the way editors dealt with the problem of French-Canadian literature. Was it "Canadian"? Was it English-Canadian if it appeared in translation? Was it right to translate it in the first place?

In the pre-Trudeau era, editors are generally aware that there is a profound dilemma here. In a 1946 anthology, J.D. Robins publishes a few works in translation, but laments that he can't publish them in French because "to our shame" few anglophones would be able to read them.[10] In a 1950 anthology, editor Desmond Pacey refuses to cater to unilingual readers by including translated French work because this would be "more of an insult to our French-speaking countrymen than to omit them altogether." He added that the literatures had evolved separately, and that it would be wrong to impose an "artificial unity" on them. Most anthologists, Sugars notes, did include Quebec work in translation, but always with a good deal of unease. Few tried to claim that there was a single Canadian literature which happened to exist in two languages.

With the need to counter rising Quebec nationalism in the 1960's, however, the federal government moved toward consciously bicultural policies. The academics followed suit, suddenly filling anthologies with translated work and "questionably... promoting what they considered to be the essential likeness of the two cultures through an affirmation of the similarities of their literary products."[11]

She also notices— and this is something which did not occur before Trudeau— that some scholars began to feel that "once translated or 'Englished,' these particular French-Canadian texts are just that, 'English'— and hence unproblematically part of an English-Canadian canon."[12]

A similar impulse lay behind the French immersion movement: that if the cultures could get to "know" each other, they would find that they were alike. Indeed, one could simply decide that they *were* alike. Canada could exist. This is the essence of wishful thinking. "Isn't it worrisome," writes Christian Dufour, "that we can no longer see, or want to see, that a massively anglophone population far from Quebec cannot become bilingual?... It will be difficult to attenuate, even mildly, Canadian idealism. That would oblige Canadians and Quebeckers to confront painful realities which they have carefully avoided."[13]

Twenty-five years' experience of French immersion has tended to show that the common sense of the Lowers and the Dufours was on the mark. Although immersion students acquire a certain hothouse fluency in the language, most lack confidence "due to a lack of contact with francophones"[14] when they try to talk to a native speaker. In a recent study of 127 immersion students in Alberta, two-thirds never read in French for pleasure outside of school.[15] It is a little like Italo Calvino's image of a city made up entirely of plumbing. The toilets flush, but there is no floor or building around them.

It is natural for anglophones of good will to want to do something to "solve" the language problem. But the solution, if there is one, does not lie so much in a few English Canadians learning to speak French as it does in all English Canadians coming to *recognize* French. By that I mean that French must have constitutional and de facto recognition as being in every way the equal of the English language in this country, and not merely the object of a sort of patronizing folkloric survival. It also means that English Canadians cease criticizing and second-guessing the language laws and policies of Quebec. As early as 1971, Ronald Sutherland put his finger on the problem with Trudeau's approach:

> If a genuine feeling of cultural security is to be created once and for all in Quebec... [it] must become an officially unilingual, French-language province... After all, the other nine provinces are essentially unilingual. Whatever the glories of bilingualism, so long as it smacks of necessary accommodation it will be regarded in Quebec as a threat to the French language... To the average English Canadian, bilingualism means acquiring a second language; at the moment, to many French Canadians it means the likelihood of losing a first one.[16]

To be at risk of losing your first language is one of the great human traumas, particularly in the modern world where language plays a larger role than before in the definition of human identity. In an attempt to describe Quebec's particular dilemma, Charles Taylor has written an essay called "Why Do Nations Have to Become States?" where he puts this uniquely modern valuing of language in a historic context.

He begins by going back several centuries, when earlier systems of communal belonging, particularly religious and hierarchial ones, began to erode. This coincided with the modern idea of the individual, whose "humanity is something we each discover in ourselves." Politically speaking, a group of such individuals living in a political unit was seen as having inalienable rights, including the right to self-rule.[17]

From about the end of the eighteenth century, "language" began to become important. This was related to a new idea, that the individual was not only endowed with rights, but was also unique. To establish a unique identity, a person "needs a horizon of meaning, which can only be provided by some allegiance, group membership, cultural tradition. He needs, in the broadest sense, a language in which to ask and answer the questions of ultimate significance."[18]

By "ask and answer," Taylor is alluding to ideas he has developed elsewhere, to the effect that human beings do not develop an identity by sitting alone in a room and thinking about it. Identity is *dialogic*, and can only become real when tested against other human beings whose reaction we value.

But, out of the swirl of humanity, how can we know with whom to be in dialogue? It should be those with whom we have the easiest and most accurate communication— those who speak the same language. "Since the Romantic insight is that we need a language in the broadest sense in order to discover our humanity, and that this language is something we have access to through our community, it is natural that the community defined by natural language should become one of the most important poles of identification... Hence nationalism, the singling out of linguistic nationality as the paradigm pole of self-identity, is part of this modern drive to emancipation."[19]

We can see the traces of romantic thinking in the way that people today describe the trauma of linguistic assimilation as a loss of intimacy with nature and life. Eva Hoffman, for example, describes what it cost her to leave behind not so much Poland, but the Polish language, in order to become a Canadian:

> The words I learn now (in English) don't stand for things in the same unquestioned way they did in my native tongue. "River" in Polish was a vital sound, energized with the essence... of my being immersed in rivers. "Rivers" in English is cold— a word without an aura. It has no accumulated associations for me... it does not evoke.

It is not only the word which is damaged, but the thing itself. "When I see a river now... [it] remains a thing, absolutely other, absolutely unbending to the grasp of my mind."[20]

An English Canadian who learns French as a second language does *not* experience what Hoffman is talking about. In order to understand the pain she describes, that person must also resolve never to speak English again.

Many French Canadians, of course, literally lost their language once they moved to Toronto or Vancouver. But in the last 30 years, more and more attention has been focussed on a related matter: the deterioration of French within Quebec itself, under the continual pressure of the English language. Writing in 1964, the poet Fernand Ouellette decries this forced "bilingualism":

> In Montreal, the bilingual milieu par excellence, our brains each day absorb an incalculable number of visual sensations [signs in English] and auditory ones [scraps of conversation], a quantity of words and strange syntactic turns. If our conscious knowledge of French is virtually nil, if we continually accept camouflaged English [here he is referring to people who use anglicisms without knowing it], we are all the more

helpless before this invasion by a language which daily impregnates our consciousness.[21]

In the end, Ouellette foresees a literal collapse of resistance, where francophones will begin to speak English because it will have become easier for them than speaking their native language. Today, this kind of rhetoric may seem extreme if not ridiculous; but the Quebec of the 1960's was an absurdly colonized society where "union leaders would have to bargain in English with management on behalf of a work force that was 100 per cent francophone."[22]

Quebec was, evidently, very far from being the polity imagined by the Romantic philosophers, in which speakers of French would prefer each other because of the clarity and ease of communicating in their own language. Ouellette, remembering his childhood, says that "many of my friends either didn't know the French word corresponding to an object, or else they knew the English word... Our thirst for words has not been slaked."[23]

This rhetoric is not as peculiar as it seems. Ouellette is simply saying that people didn't know the names of different trees, or kitchen implements, or what particular bird had landed on the windowsill. So they said "tree" or "bird" or "whachamacallit" instead. Even though the situation is much better now than then, I have often been somewhat shaken at the inability of well-educated Quebeckers to supply me with the word for "sparrow" or "sieve" when I point out the object in question. It is unnerving when an auto mechanic doesn't know how to say "bumper" in his own language, and goes consulting around the garage in the hope that somebody else might.

According to Taylor, philosophers are able to argue that languages, as an expression of human communities, can have "rights" analogous to those of an individual. In particular, a language has the three rights of "expression, realization and recognition."[24]

Expression means "cultural" expression, that the group has the freedom to make art and public institutions in its language so as to "continually re-create" itself.

Realization means that the language is used "for the whole gamut of human purposes," including the latest developments in technology and learning. Otherwise, the language of these realizations "will inevitably be a foreign one."

Recognition has to do with the relationship between this linguistic community and its neighbours. Just as individuals need to be recognized for "what we are," so a language community requires "an acceptance by the world community that one counts for something, has something to say to the world, and is among those addressed by others— the need to exist as a people on the world stage."[25]

Of these three rights, the only one which existed for Quebec during the first century after the Conquest was "expression." This, perhaps, is why Fernand Dumont developed his theory that Quebec during this time survived by imagining itself as a "cultural nation" rather than a "political nation."

During this time, "realization" was out of the question because Quebec's economy was under the control of anglophones. This is perhaps the place to mention the curious fact that the British forbade French vessels to trade up the St. Lawrence for nearly a century after the conquest. When the first French vessel returned in 1855, a little freighter named the *Capricieuse*, crowds lined up along the river to cheer, and Octave Crémazie wrote a poem in its honour.

It is a charming image, but the 100-year absence of France had dreadfully practical consequences. This was the century during which France experienced the industrial revolution. Little of this language was transmitted to Quebec. When the habitant farmers began to come to the cities looking for work in the English factories, they adopted English words for the machines, the tools, and the products they made. The coming twentieth century did not exist in Quebec French. "For a goodly number of French Canadians, French is no longer the daily language," declared the Ligue des droits du français in 1913. "In certain areas, such as commerce and industry, it has been completely rejected."[26]

As for the third level, *recognition*— well, French words weren't even printed on the money people spent each day. And as we have seen, French speakers were also rendered invisible in the English-Canadian imagination. "Tact and tolerance are the very qualities that have invariably been in short supply among the English of the New World," wrote Arthur Lower. "They might have made at least a Switzerland out of Canada and they have (instead) created an Austria-Hungary."[27]

With the coming of the Quiet Revolution, Quebec society burst out of its old religious and political strait-jacket. Confident young fonctionnaires descended on Ottawa, paving the way for the Trudeau revolution; in Quebec, the Parti Québécois swept the anglophone business oligarchy aside. Political power was wrenched away from the clergy, even as church attendance plummetted. L'École des hautes études commerciales sent students to business school at Harvard, hiring them back immediately as professors. A massive transfer of knowledge took place, and Quebec's economy rapidly modernized.

Modernizing the language, however, was not so easy. The Quebec patois, although shorn of precise words for traditional things, and without words for new things, was after all the tough survivor of centuries of oppression. It had vivid folkloric expressions, and more importantly, it embodied a certain direct, no-nonsense way of being. "'Chus lette, mais j'pogne" says a T-shirt. "I'm ugly, but I get what I want!" It's not only the sentiment which embodies a particular history, but the words themselves. The verb "pogner" does not exist in standard French, and the average Parisian is unlikely to understand that "chus" means "je suis" or that "lette" means "laid" (ugly).

A number of artists, of whom Michel Tremblay is the best known, triumphantly proved that joual could be the vehicle of a new literature.

Not that it had gone unnoticed before; you can see passages of joual dialogue in *Charles Guérin*. But a group of modern writers, whose founding text was Jacques Renaud's scrappy, violent and anomie-ridden 1963 novel *Le Cassé* (Broke City), used joual for narrative as well as dialogue. These writers, who also included Claude Jasmin, insisted that joual was the only authentic language of Quebec.

In the theatre, Tremblay inspired writers such as René-Daniel Dubois, a cultivated fellow who uses virtually uncut joual in the dialogues of his plays and film scripts. Indeed, his most famous film is called *Being At Home With Claude*. The defiantly English title reflects the fact that joual speakers routinely lard their speech with great chunks of English; Dubois claims that, too, as part of the patrimony of Quebec's ugly little language that gets what it wants.

Parallel to this, however, there was a movement to restore a correct French equal to the demands of a modern society. A lot of people were acutely pained by the "truth" of the voices Tremblay created. They never again wanted to hear the waitress Thérèse in *En pièces détachées*:

> Un grill cheese, un ordre de toasts, deux cafés! Un cherry coke! Une tarte au citron, un verre de lait!... Un pepper steak pas de piments, un ordre de sperridzes [spareribs]! Un chicken in the basket...[28]

The novelist Jacques Renaud himself explained the paradox: "Joual is the language both of submission and revolt, of anger and impotence. It's a non-language, a denunciation."[29]

There is nothing surprising, of course, in a language borrowing words from neighbouring languages. But joual does more than that. As translator David Homel has remarked,[30] it often borrows the *grammar* of English, as when someone says "Il est sur le chomage" (He's "on" unemployment), instead of "au chomage." Another example is: "Elle l'a pitché dehors" (She pitched him out). No Latin language ends a sentence with a preposition like "dehors," or ever could. Put another way, these are not

French sentences; they are English sentences using French words— when they aren't using English words like "pitché," of course.

The problem didn't begin yesterday. In 1807 a travelling Englishman, John Lambert, noticed that Canadiens were pronouncing the final letters of words, a practice "perhaps acquired in the course of 50 years communication with the British settlers."[31] A little later, Alexis de Tocqueville was puzzled by the "strange turns of phrase" in Quebec newspapers, and repulsed by the language of lawyers, mixed as it was with "strangenesses and English locutions. They say that a man is 'chargé' ten louis to mean that on lui demande dix louis."[32] In 1851, a French traveller, Jean Jacques Ampère, was astonished to see a sign reading "sirop de toute description." In French, "sirop" should be pluralized. It seems, wrote Ampère, that "the plural disappears where it is absent in the rival language... The conquest of grammar after that of arms!"[33]

French speakers were yielding their pride with their plurals. François-Xavier Garneau recalls in his history that when Quebec was given a legislature in 1791, the English members— representing four per cent of the population— demanded that French not be spoken in the assembly. To everybody's astonishment, a local lawyer, P.L. Panet, agreed. "Is not this country a British possession?" he argued. "Is not the English language that of the sovereign and the British legislature?"

Panet himself spoke English imperfectly. He was willing to accept his own marginalization. But as yet, his "reasoning, which had more servility than logic in it, convinced none of his compatriots."[34]

As time went by, more and more Quebeckers adopted Panet's servility until it became so general as not to be noticed. English became the language of the public square, and the French spoken in Quebec began its long downward spiral toward the angry, bitten-off syllabics of joual.

So the linguistic awakening during the Quiet Revolution was a confused and angry one. For every Michel Tremblay celebrating joual, there was an angry poet like Fernand Ouellette lamenting the poverty of the "franglais" he had learned as a child.

As Quebec professionalized itself, linguists like Jean-Marc Léger appeared and gave voice to another problem, which they called "translation." This was not the translating which lets a culture open out onto the world. It was the violent, force-fed everyday task of translating the multitude of English posters, voices, shop signs, newspapers, and television channels which inundated Quebeckers. In his view, modes of thinking and syntax peculiar to the French language could not possibly survive this never-ending, compulsory "translation."[35]

Léger's argument goes back to the roots of modern philology, when philosophers like Schleiermacher first articulated the notion that "every language is a particular mode of thought, and what is cogitated in one language can never be repeated in the same way in another."[36]

Modern linguists have shown that these early observations are essentially correct, which gives force to the complaints of Quebeckers today. However, some philosophers went too far, arguing for an idealized purity and a refusal of all foreign words. Strains of this romantic hysteria can sometimes be heard in the denunciations of English written by extreme nationalists in Quebec. Ouellette himself adopted some of the odder thinking of Herder and Fichte when he argued that it is unnatural to be bilingual. "When a child receives a word, it is a symbiosis," wrote Ouellette. "Whoever grows up in a bilingual milieu lives in mental confusion... his mental structures are weakened. It's not surprising that Rémy de Gourmont has written that 'bilingual people are almost always inferior people.'"[37]

This kind of thing got so out of hand that Marie-Claire Blais devoted a satirical novel to it. It's usually called *St. Lawrence Blues* in English, but the French title gets you closer to the flavour: *Un joualonais sa joualonie*. It satirized the infatuation of intellectuals with the "pure Quebec joual" spoken by petty grifters and race-track touts.

Behind all this, however, there was the undeniable power of the English language. Like an iceberg in a shipping lane, it simply crushed or elbowed aside everything in its way. In 1825 Augustin-Norbert Morin, who would later become a rebel, looked on in amazement when it was decreed that all trials would be in English. "Speak a foreign language, [our litigants] will be told; use an idiom you haven't learned... Go home; learn, somehow or other, this magical language which decides all claims and shortens all trials."[38]

A century-and-a-half later, Michel Tremblay would return to the idea of the "magical" power of English in the character of Marcel, who has lost his mind as a young man and has been locked up in an asylum for 20 years. Marcel believes that when he puts on his sunglasses, he is endowed with the power of invisibility— and the power to speak English.

> Go on, speak English, you'll see, I understand it all. In the hospital, with my glasses I disappeared into the walls, then they could go ahead and speak all the English they wanted, I understood it all! It's my power does that! With my power I can do all kinds of things, mommy! I can make things appear and disappear!... but sometimes they stay! Sometimes they stay, mommy, and then I'm afraid![39]

The English language has, evidently, "stayed"; it is the language of the hospital in which Quebec is confined. This is a literary way of saying that there are three hundred million of us to six million of them, which of course is not our fault; but it does create a psychological reality which francophones must deal with. As theatre critic Paul Lefebvre has written, "What Québécois has not dreamed of one day ceasing to speak French, of being re-born into the great family of the English-speaking majority?"[40]

Lefebvre wrote these remarks in connection with a one-man show called *The Dragonfly of Chicoutimi*, which premiered in 1995 at the Festival des Amériques in Montreal. The play embodies the problem we have been discussing, because the author, Larry Tremblay, had originally intended to write it in French, but found that when he visualized the character, he heard him speaking English.

The character, Gaston Talbot, has only recently recovered his speech after being aphasic since childhood. Tremblay had originally imagined this as a standard Freudian trauma: Gaston had been traumatized by his role in a childhood accident which killed another little boy.

The story took on greater interest when Tremblay's subconscious kept giving him Gaston *speaking English*. What would cause a francophone to lose his speech, and then wake up one day speaking another language?

Tremblay decided to write the play in English even though his own command of the language is imperfect. The result is a very moving, roughly poetic text. Gaston awakens one morning from a dream— able to speak. In the dream he was once again a child in Chicoutimi sucking on his favourite popsicle, "a white popsicle, a kind of coconut taste but so artificial that it was impossible to find out the stuff they use." Then

> the popsicle simply disappeared
> ...like a bird or a flower is made disappeared
> by the quick hands of a magician
> I wasn't impressed at all by this disparition
> I said
> my popsicle disappeared so what
> I said that in English
> and I wasn't at all impressed
> by the fact I said that in English
> I was a child
> with an adult body
> speaking in English
> so what.[41]

Except that he soon realizes he no longer has his own face. "There is always a but/ his face oh his face/ this face was not mine/ a strange mix in fact... the face of the boy in my dream/ which is supposed to be mine/ looked exactly like a face of a Picasso."[42]

What Jacques Godbout evoked with satire in *Les Têtes à Papineau* comes to Larry Tremblay as poetry. But the shock is profound in both cases. To lose one's language is to lose one's "face," to no longer be the person that you were.

CHAPTER SEVEN

Quelle chaleur!
J'en viens presque à rêver de l'hiver
Je me suis arrêté près d'ici
une poussière dans l'oeil
à la pointe de l'ancien hôtel de ville
se tient en équilibre un oiseau noir
il s'évente lentement pour se rafraîchir
les ailes déployés.

What heat!
It almost makes me dream of winter.
I stopped not far from here,
to get the dust out of my eye.
At the corner of the old city hall
A black bird teeters on the wind
Airing himself, refreshing himself
His wings spread wide.
— G. Boyer, 1988
Plaque attached to building at corner of St. Laurent and Laurier

Much of this book has been about the past. And yet we often hear today that the past, especially in Quebec, has been swept away.

There is no doubt, on a superficial level, that this is true. Children in Quebec play with the same extruded plastic toys (invariably stamped with English names and instructions) as children throughout the western world. The consumption of American movies has doubled in the last 20 years, and now occupies over 80 per cent of Quebec screen time. Sociologists agonize over the baby-boomer bulge denying job opportunities to the young, just as they do in Toronto and Vancouver. Kids in black shirts with earrings punched through their lips loiter on downtown street corners.

"The truth is," wrote Jacques Godbout 20 years ago, "our ideas come from France, but our myths, fictions, credit cards and comfort come from the United States."[1] Twenty years ago, on visits to Montreal, I could still find bière d'épinette (spruce beer) on the shelves of corner stores; today there's nothing but Mountain Dew and Tahiti Treat.

But the French "ideas" are still there. The ancient Catholic battle against materialism is still being waged. And there are still absolute ideas of the good— particularly the good of the community— which escape the levelling grasp of marketplace ideology. There is a bistro down the street from my home where people read Argentine novels and talk politics passionately. One rarely hears ecstatic tales of solid brass shower heads or purpleheart inlays in the front hall. Not a few former Montrealers have come fleeing back from Vancouver or Calgary because they missed the conversation.

Above all, the idea that Quebeckers are a "people," a living culture, is widely embraced. This directly affects the kind of life that is lived in Montreal. Perhaps a comparison with Toronto, which embodies so many Canadian assumptions, will illustrate the difference.

One can begin with the *public* presence or absence of artists, whose task, in the words of singer Marie-Claire Séguin, is to "name" a place. Toronto has not much been loved by its citizens or artists; it has not, in the sense Séguin intends, been "named" by those who live in it.

The passage of poetry quoted at the beginning of this chapter, by way of contrast, is located on a brass plaque fixed to a building at the corner of Laurier Ave. and St. Laurent in Montreal. The city puts up any number of these plaques to commemorate places that have inspired writers. This program is the sort of thing that makes incontrovertible sense once it is placed in front of you. Why shouldn't you love your city as you love your home, and deck it with affectionate mementos?

Montreal's current blend of high and low culture is the logical outcome of its history. It has poets, but also tacky entertainment tabloids[2] wherein— a recent example— singer Nathalie Simard begs her fans to forgive her for burning down her house to defraud the insurance company.

The gleeful tackiness of Quebec's popular culture is part of a profound reflex which has permitted the French language to survive despite poor odds. It creates francophone equivalents of almost everything that exists in U.S. culture, from bluesmen who pay reverential visits to Mississippi to a wild west rodeo at rural St.-Tite. Montreal's private sector TV has its Oprah clone, Sonia Benezra, tacky game shows, and tele-romans full of extravagant emotion and ridiculous coincidence.

None of these things, however, are exact imitations. The tele-roman, for example, is a blend of soap opera and situation comedy which would confuse a television viewer accustomed to American genres. Quebec's popular culture has been shaped to suit community tastes which predate the founding of Canada. The result is a relaxed sense of at-home-ness. American culture is present, but almost invisible. Montreal's public face, the celebrities pictured on kiosques or selling pizza on TV, belong to the city.

High culture profits from this. Comedian Benoît Brière is famous for his Bell telephone commercials: hordes of people went to see him last summer in Molière's *Bourgeois Gentilhomme*.

Toronto, on the other hand, has long since chosen to live in what one québécois observer calls a "feudal" relationship with American culture. While working as a theatre critic in Toronto, I noticed that people often expressed discomfort or even embarrassment if a stage piece had a local setting. George F. Walker, whose elegantly bizarre Toronto plays have been produced around the world, and who should have become a public figure to rival Michel Tremblay, is unacknowledged. Torontonians, like English Canadians generally, are still unable to make the gestures of self-recognition.

By way of example, it seems normal and natural to us to prefer American television, but on an international scale Quebec's preference for its own popular culture is far more "normal." "Our public still vastly prefers its own [TV] shows to anybody else's," says Michèle Fortin, director of the French-language service of the CBC. "But this is true everywhere in the world, with the exception of [English] Canada and possibly New Zealand, which are special cases."

Underpinning the difference between Montreal and Toronto is an idea which English Canada has adopted from the United States, and which seems to go back to the thinking of John Locke as expressed in the U.S. Constitution: that the modern individual is self-creating, free from the past. There is an irony here. If English Canada today believes in this doctrine, with its concomitant mistrust of community, it is precisely because it has inherited it from the past.

If we go back to the beginning, we find that important early decisions were made in the light of this doctrine. Our first literary writers, for example, mistrusted imagination. In the words of Carl Ballstadt, they "regarded literature in which the fancy was given free reign as being inappropriate to a new country."[3] A community cannot come into existence unless it dares to imagine the world on its own terms.

We have already seen how, by contrast, early writers in Quebec seized on imagination as a primary value for the literature of the new society. It is remarkable how consistently the two cultures continue to live out these early decisions. One day in the early 1980's, doing a story on the National Theatre School in Montreal, I learned that the English graduating class was doing *Romeo and Juliet*, while the French graduating class was doing a play it had written itself. This was, I learned to my surprise, the consistent behaviour of the two national groups in the school; so much so that nobody found it remarkable or noteworthy.

The view of the Romantic philosophers was that the confidence to be creative arises when one lives in a community that shares a common "language" in the large sense of shared values and goals. In English Canada, where the shared language is weak, creative people often speak in terms similar to those of Frederick Philip Grove: that being a writer is somewhat like groping in a dark room, or crying out and not receiving an answer.

The contrasting situation in Quebec is evident in the following remarks by Montreal playwright Michel March Bouchard: "What I like here is that people like our culture. I wish that for Toronto. When I'm there [in Toronto] it feels like Buenos Aires, a kind of cultural Third World. You look out the hotel window and all you see is posters for *Phantom of the Opera*. English Canada doesn't love its artists the way we do. And that love gives us confidence and means."[4]

This is not to suggest that Toronto is a dull or uninteresting city. Quite the contrary. Torontonians are wealthy, they have access to the best culture from everywhere else, they fight political battles and feel very involved with their city in a "civic" way. They don't *seem* to miss the emotional depth of a reflective, living culture because they have access to any manner of other distractions. The descendants of Lorne Murchison still dream of imperialism; but instead of longing for England, they meet in Joe Allen's on the Danforth and trade dreams of writing sitcom scripts in Los Angeles.

One can be happy under anaesthetic, so long as things go well. But when there is a crisis— such as the fiscal crisis that began in 1988 and is far from ended— "stunted and vulgar"[5] politicians (in political scientist Jack McLeod's phrase) quickly come to the fore. In the absence of a widespread, functioning local culture, a people risks finding itself governed by men and women who do not understand or care about the expressiveness of their community. The contrast with Quebec is obvious: vocal support for culture, in good times and bad, is a prerequisite to getting elected to anything.

A criticism of Quebec which is frequently expressed is that shared values at a certain point become suffocating because they inhibit individual expression. Typical are the remarks of Toronto academic Robert Wallace, who was living in Quebec at the time of René Lévesque's death. "When I went out in the street that morning I knew something was wrong even before seeing a newspaper. People walking along were visibly depressed. For the first time I knew what the expression 'a city in mourning' meant."[6]

Wallace discovered that he did "not find this alluring." It struck him as un-modern, the mark of a closed society. Similar expressions of alarm can often be heard among the English-Canadian intelligentsia when Quebec politicians talk about the "social role" of the artist. Visions of regimentation and state censors begin to dance in their heads.

In reality, however, the opposite seems to be the case. Quebec in my experience supports a wider range of views and a greater public spontaneity than English Canada. And I think this is why: the building of a community does not imply a monotonous similarity of views. It requires only a positive disposition toward the community. In England (by way of example), social critics with opposite ideas are united by nothing except a profound attachment to England. This permits a ferocious public exchange of views in which the participants do not seem to be harmed.

Something similar is evident in Quebec. Newspaper articles reflect a range of views, some of them eccentric, exceedingly unfashionable, and occasionally offensive, which would disconcert a reader in Toronto or Vancouver. A politician may abandon his script and say something peremptory off the top of his head, leaving the English media howling and the French media shrugging their collective shoulders.

Even as I write, the Montreal *Gazette* is gasping in indignation because prominent Radio-Canada announcer Bernard Derome said unflattering things about a few countries while their athletes were parading at the Olympic Games. The English media made lists of countries to see if they could accuse Derome of racism. The French media, on the other hand, have decided that he got tired of the incessant high-mindedness of the Olympics and let off a little steam.

I got an insight into these different mind-sets of the two cultures during a conversation one day with Louise Baillargeon, the head of the Quebec Film and Television Producers' Association. She said that during meetings with her anglo-Canadian confrères in Toronto, she will sometimes "say something off the top of my head, something outrageous, just to break up all the politeness and get things moving. They are always shocked by this, but it seems to me the most natural thing in the world."

I don't think that this oft-remarked difference between Quebeckers and Canadians has anything to do with "Latin" or "Anglo-Saxon" temperaments. It has to do with whether you live in a community or not. English Canada, in my view, prizes politeness and indirectness of speech because it lacks that profound communal grounding which enables people to speak freely. In a society of atomized individuals, each person is dreadfully vulnerable and everybody walks on eggs.

To return, then, to the death of René Lévesque. The city was, indeed, in mourning, because Lévesque embodied the love of Quebec which is the bedrock of the community. But that certainly does not imply that he was some sort of Svengali with whose opinions nobody dared disagree— as the results of the referendum attest.

The paradox, then, is that the individual finds freedom of expression only through committing to the group. In Charles Taylor's terms, the pure individual (or monad) of the Enlightenment philosophers does not exist. To spend one's life seeking this chimera is to forego living in community. "That is what is self-defeating in modes of contemporary culture that concentrate on self-fulfillment in opposition to the demands of society... [and] which shut out history and the bonds of solidarity."[7]

Quebec is not, however, the ideal national community. It is still under a great deal of stress because of the unresolved issue of its relationship with Canada. This, I think, exaggerates the comfortable solidarity of a settled community and creates an unhealthy tendency to mass consensus about television programs, filmmakers, athletes— whoever or whatever is held to embody Quebec at a given moment.

This would explain, for example, the extraordinary flocking of the public to television series like *Les filles de Caleb* (1991), which recounted the life of a young woman struggling for personal freedom in the closed rural society of the last century. The story was well told and not without modest literary qualities; the programs were beautifully shot and well-acted. But it was not such a masterpiece that it should have attracted nearly half the population of the province to their TV sets each night!

This popular unanimity dates back to the introduction of television. It has imprinted certain characters, such as Antonine Maillet's *La Sagouine*, or the bizarre Moman and Popa of the suburban comedy *La Petite Vie*, on the public imagination. Some commentators have suggested that the arrival of television, which coincided with the Quiet Revolution, helped to define the collective personality of Quebec at that crucial moment in its history.

In some circumstances— and one can't always predict which ones— this makes it difficult to be critical of popular personalities. This came home to me one evening in the Théâtre St.-Denis, where there was a ceremony to commemorate the best Quebec pop music of the year. An a capella group, La bande magnetik, did a Swingle Singers-type sampling of the year's top ten Quebec pop songs. It was an ambitious undertaking, and it failed in a cacophony of missed bridges and dropped melodies. My first impulse, as a good individualist, was to make fun of their ineptness with a well-chosen bon mot. But I was stopped by the look in the eyes of the lady standing beside me. With a stiff, rueful smile she turned and said: "C'est... speciale, hm?" Then she joined the house in a belated but warm round of applause.

On another occasion, at a handicrafts fair in the Place Bonaventure, I expressed curiosity about an immense photograph of an elderly man in the weaving pavilion. "Oh," explained a young woman proudly, "he was the father of Quebec artistic weaving!"

For an artist of major talent, such as filmmaker Denys Arcand, this sort of thing can become insufferable. Once a separatist, he has now become politically agnostic because he has noticed that artists are often suborned into a collective role rather than being allowed to pursue personal inspiration. "It's not claustrophobic, exactly," Arcand told me in an interview, "but you feel people put too much on your shoulders. You *become* Quebec cinema, which is something no one can accept and live with."

Many artists feel Arcand's frustrations, but very few of them would say that the virtual invisibility of the artist in English Canada is an appealing alternative. Quebec's artists prefer to re-shape the Quebec environment so that it is less volatile, but retains its underlying respect for the role of creative people. Even Arcand is dismayed by the alternative model of human relations offered by American, and increasingly by global, society. In his recent film *Unidentified Human Remains*, he examines the sameness of young people throughout the western world today. "We're in a time when western cultures are less and less different: MTV, the same music, the same dances. Everybody has been thrown into the media blender."

For Arcand, the Quebec generation now approaching 50 years of age— the group of university teachers portrayed in his earlier film, *Le Déclin de l'empire américain*— was the last to enjoy a coherent group identity. Gathered at a farm for the weekend, they eat, flirt, and fornicate together. But mostly they talk, and if one of them refers to Bishop Bourget (an early builder of the Catholic Church in Quebec) nobody needs an explanation.

It's a measure of the real difference between the Quebec cultural model and that of North America, that a Hollywood attempt to remake *Le Déclin* in English failed. The sticking point, says Arcand, is that American university teachers are locked into a competitive model which makes the life portrayed in the film implausible.

For this reason, many talented artists who could have made a career elsewhere have elected to stay in Quebec. Prominent among them is theatre director Robert Lepage, who rebuffed inquiries from the Paris

Opera and filmmaker Ingmar Bergman's suggestion that Lepage succeed him at the head of his Stockholm theatre company.

Lepage made his reputation with works such as *The Dragon's Trilogy* and *Polygraphe*, which were intimately inspired by the sounds, the people, and the landscape of Quebec City where he grew up. He has also been successful with "international" works such as *Tectonic Plates*, but today feels that these represent a false step, because they were calculated to appeal to a global audience.

"Michel Tremblay says it's sad to see Quebec artists creating work that is designed to move people abroad," says Robert Lepage. "I agree with him. The trick is to be local. *That* is what will move people abroad. An artist must talk about what he knows."

For every Arcand chafing against nationalism, there is a Tremblay or a Lepage who is nourished by it. But all of these artists, it is safe to say, are fatigued with the endless political tension which prevents Quebec— and Canada— from moving forward into the future.

Another difficulty which faces Quebec today, however, comes from its falling birth rate. In common with English Canada and many developed countries, Quebec relies on immigration to stabilize a population that otherwise would decline.

Immigrants to English Canada learn English, in line with the practice of unilingualism which has evolved in modern nation states whether they claim to be "nationalistic" or not (let's not waste time over the absurdity of English Canada pretending to be "bilingual").

Logically speaking, immigrants to Quebec should learn French, which is the official language of the province. But in fact a majority insist on learning English, following self-interest by choosing the dominant language of both Canada and North America.

There has been a noisy battle of statistics as to how many Quebec immigrants become anglophone, and how long it would take for them decisively to shift the province's demographic balance against the French language. But most people agree that more than half of them— even today— are still choosing English (in the past some estimates were as high as 90 per cent). Simple arithmetic dictates that if the figure is more than 50 per cent, immigration will, however slowly, cause English to spread and French to retreat.

In 1977 the infamous Bill 101 was passed in order to deal decisively with the matter. It obliged all immigrants to Quebec— except those from English-speaking countries— to educate their children in French.

This was clearly a violation of individual freedom of choice, as understood by classic liberals. But on the other hand, to respect the immigrant's "individual" choice seemed recklessly to endanger the long-term survival of the French community.

This was the underlying conflict sensed by Oscar Dunn nearly a hundred years ago. Recently, political theorists like Germany's Jurgen Habermas[8] have made the matter explicit: a liberal state cannot guarantee the survival of a minority language. To do so means legally enforcing statements such as, "French will be spoken in this country a century from now." Assuming such enforcement to be possible, argues Habermas, it would violate the individual human rights of future generations.

Liberal arguments of this sort caused the Supreme Court of Canada to strike down Bill 101. But Quebec used its authority to override court decisions touching on its vital interests, and Bill 101 still stands today. Quebec's anglophones never cease trying to weaken it, or Canada's media to use it as grist in their tiresome campaign to attach the word "fascist" to Quebec.

A related threat to Quebec's culture is federal multiculturalism policy. The policy, in the words of McGill theologian Gregory Baum, states that Canada is a country with two official languages but a multitude of cultures, all equally valued. "Canada no longer sees itself as a country founded on the union of two civilizations," so that Canadians can "no longer tell their history through the foundation of la Nouvelle France, the conflict with the native people, the British conquest, and the search of the British and French communities to find a political compromise or mutual agreement culminating in Confederation in 1867."

Quebec has not accepted this policy, adds Baum, because it "takes away its history and collective identity."[9] Instead, the province has created a policy called inter-culturalism, which calls upon immigrants to recognize that a "host culture" (culture d'accueil) already exists in Quebec, and that immigrants are to situate themselves within it. In exchange, their culture will be treated respectfully by Quebeckers.

The idea of inter-culturalism has certainly been attacked. It has been suggested that its roots are in the Jansenist nationalism of France, which declares that the founders of a nation are especially privileged to set its terms, and that those who arrive later must accept them without exception.

I personally have never seen what is the problem with this "Jansenist" nationalism, apart from the ruthlessness with which it may have been applied in the European past. But surely even today no country is willing to overturn its founding values simply because immigrants don't care for them. Perhaps the matter becomes clearer if we turn the question around: in what sense, exactly, *can* immigrants change a culture which is already in place? At best, only very gradually and probably without touching its core values and principles at all.

The CEQ, the Quebec Teacher's Union, has written the most common-sense statement on this matter that I have come across. "Any Quebecker, even one who wishes it were otherwise, is affected and concerned by the fact that the society in which he lives has its own peculiar characteristics and a peculiar dynamic of social life. To be a Quebecker it is not necessary to belong to the French-Canadian ethnic group, but to be a Quebecker regardless of one's ethnic affiliation is something quite different from being a Canadian or American."[10]

Notice particularly the phrase, "even one who wishes it were otherwise." This is a simple statement of reality, a refusal of the "wishful" thinking that lies behind incoherent ideas such as multiculturalism.

Federal policies which tend to obliterate Quebec's distinctiveness reflect an underlying reality: that English speakers in Canada have never demonstrated solidarity with the French in matters pertaining to the protection of their culture. Every initiative on behalf of the French language, from its re-establishment in the Quebec civil service in 1910, to attempts in the summer of 1996 to re-activate the Commission de la protection de la langue française, have been met with ferocious resistance from English speakers.

This would be a different country if one could point to even a single example of a situation where English speakers had considered a proposed measure on behalf of French, and said: "Yes, that seems fair and reasonable."

In some cases English speakers have retroactively come to appreciate the justice of certain measures. Few today would argue that the Quebec government should carry on its business in English. And today, much to its credit, a thoughtful minority of the Quebec anglophone community— including the Montreal *Gazette*— has acknowledged that it is both right and proper that immigrants to a French-speaking province be made to educate their children in French.

But this latter acknowledgement comes nearly 20 years after the passage of Bill 101. It is an unfortunate thing, but heel-dragging and after-the-fact agreement cannot create solidarity between two parties. When *Gazette* editor Joan Fraser tried to argue during an episode of the French television show Bouillon de culture (June 2, 1996) that the two cultures in Quebec now act in mutual tolerance and cooperation, she was curtly challenged by *Le Devoir* editor Lise Bissonnette. "What we [French] have obtained was not gotten by tolerance between our peoples, but by us fighting for it inch by inch."

Stéphane Dion, Intergovernmental Affairs Minister in the current federal government, shows an appreciation of the problem when he urges Canadians to "express solidarity with Quebeckers" by putting the words "distinct society" into the country's constitution. The Reform Party's Stephen Harper replies by saying that "there is no evidence that Canadians oppose Quebeckers' struggle to survive"; that is to say, it is enough if Canadians do nothing. In Harper's view, there is no reason to express solidarity by actually helping them.

Harper concludes his thought by adding that there is "even less evidence that such a struggle is necessary."[11] That is to say, a unilingual anglophone living in Calgary is presuming to tell French Canadians that there is no need for them to struggle on behalf of their culture.

This kind of presumption is, I think, what Neil Bissoondath has called the "conqueror's mentality." That it is so widespread in Canada today demonstrates that we have not moved forward since Father Raymond Bourgault asked, 30 years ago, how "biculturalism" could be possible when the cultivated élite of English Canada refused to defend French Canada against "those among their own people who consider us to be intruders and unwelcome guests."

For Bourgault, it was not clear how a "former race of masters and a former race of subjects" could find the "sensible equality" that is necessary to make biculturalism work. He concluded that it could occur only through an act of will, "une volonté plus vigoureuse d'amitié" on both sides.[12]

Such an act of will has not occurred, and given the hardening of the English Canadian viewpoint it seems unlikely that it will. What we need to ask ourselves is: Is this failure a simple expression of Canada's history, or is it an example of inbuilt limitations in human behaviour, a touching of the outer limits of empathy? Put another way, has any country in the world managed the "act of will" necessary to the true recognition of a minority people? "The evidence that democracy almost never works in societies that are highly divided along linguistic and cultural lines is overwhelming," wrote the American magazine *Foreign Affairs* after the 1995 referendum.[13] The article listed some dozen failures, including Lebanon, Czeckoslovakia, and Cyprus.

The only three successes that can be named are Switzerland, Belgium— and Canada. Belgium is wracked by the same kind of mutual misunderstanding we see in Canada, with the historically dominated Flemish people asserting themselves against the dominant francophones, and the country proceeding willy-nilly toward informal separation of the two. In Switzerland there are four language groups which have always lived separately and make no pretense of "national unity."

One can see the same sort of scission taking shape today in Quebec. Francophones— and we are not talking only about separatists here— increasingly demand that Quebec's anglophones identify Quebec as their country. The anglophones, with increasing rage and desperation, refuse to do so.

If any part of English Canada can command sympathy in the current situation, it would be the anglophones of Quebec.

This declaration is, I admit, startling. For most of the past 200 years Quebec's anglophones were a privileged minority which exploited the French economically and dominated them in frankly racist terms.

All of the customary tools for imposing minority rule were brought to the task, principal among them being the destruction of the majority's confidence. Consider the attitude of the anglophone soldiers who bring the body of a dead French Canadian back to his village in the darkly comic novel *La Guerre, Yes Sir!* (1968). They are shocked by the festive eating and drinking that ensues during the wake, and take it upon themselves to throw the dead man's relatives out of his house:

> What kind of animals were these French Canadians? They acted like pigs in a pigsty... the skinny Anglais examined the French Canadians' double chins and their wives' flabby breasts... The subalterns remembered what they'd been taught at school. The French Canadians were

solitary, fearful, unintelligent, without a gift for government or commerce... They'd have to be taught a civilized language... not this patois.[14]

If you're over 40, you'll remember studying William Henry Drummond's poem "Little Bateese" at school. "You bad leetle boy, not moche
you care" is permanently graven in my brain. Drummond was a quintes-
sential anglo-Quebecker who preferred his French Canadians parked
behind the milk cow and speaking an English in which subversive
thought— any thought!— was impossible:

Jus' feel de muscle along hees back,
Won't geev heem moche bodder for carry pack
On de long portage, any size canoe,
Dere's not many t'ing dat boy won't do
For he's got double-joint on hees body too,
Little Bateese![15]

One even finds that most depressing colonial mark of Cain, the
colonized intellectual who internalizes the élite's unflattering portrait of
his people. Hence Louis Fréchette, author of the fierce denunciation of
Voltaire quoted in an earlier chapter, obsequiously admired Drummond
for making the French Canadian of his doggerel poems "good, sweet,
friendly, his heart full of native poetry" albeit in "a language not his own
and which he only half speaks."[16]

The Quiet Revolution quickly turned the tables on Quebec's
anglophones, and they certainly had it coming to them.

But once stripped of a power never justified by their numbers,
English-speaking Quebeckers have demonstrated an authentic attachment to the province. Many of them feel like strangers in English Canada
because they have absorbed some of the attitude, body language and spirit
of Quebec. They are, in fact, the Quebeckers described in the teachers'
association presentation quoted earlier: certainly not ethnically French,

they nonetheless "are something quite different from being a Canadian or an American."

I confess that I have had the greatest difficulty in understanding this. Many of these anglo-Quebeckers do not speak French; or, speaking it, they do not demonstrate any particular interest in French culture. But they are fiercely attached to the place and do not wish to live anywhere else. Typical is the dentist who one day described to me, in very moving terms, the joy and relief she felt on returning to Montreal after having fled to Toronto some years earlier. Looking out her office window— which overlooks a still very English portion of Sherbrooke Street— she remarked that Montreal was "alive" for her in a way no other place could be.

The reality which has marked these anglophones is very difficult to describe. It comes down to the details of behaviour of the French, who of course are the majority and set the tone of life. There is the "mimique" or shape given to the mouth muscles by a lifetime of speaking French, which enables shopkeepers to decide which language to speak to a customer before the customer has said anything. There is the curious "third way of behaving" between francophone men and women as described by Nancy Huston, an Albertan who recently won a Governor General's award for an essay written in French. There is the greater attention to clothing and comportment, the mania for smoking, the different unspoken rules for intimate distance around a person, the slightly different facial expressions which convey astonishment or compassion... the multitude of nuances which only anthropologists can hope to pull into the full daylight of description.

At the same time, very few of Quebec's anglophones actually live "in" the French world which surrounds them. There are powerful if subtle forces which pull even bilingual people back into their own linguistic communities. If you don't spend very many hours a day in the other culture, you'll be vague on who's who and what the conventions are. Consider this episode from Colleen Curran's comic novel *Something*

Drastic. It's New Year's Eve. The narrator and her friend are considering what to watch on TV. "She says if we were politically correct Quebec Canadians, we'd watch *ByeBye*, that French comedy show looking back at the year, and we'd pretend we understood all the in jokes. But we're not gonna do that, we're gonna watch the ball drop at Times Square, as bad as it can be..."

The conclusion which imposes itself is a difficult one. But it seems to be true that English Quebeckers, however deeply marked by the French, however honest their affection for the French, still hold themselves apart from them. They do not wish to *be* French. They have no interest in undergoing the trauma of losing their native language, of seeing their "face" turned into "a face of Picasso."

One can speculate whether, in an independent Quebec that was economically secure and sure of itself, a place could be made for an English-speaking minority which sincerely wished to live in Quebec without becoming ethnically French. The problem posed by this situation would be exactly the same as the problem posed by the French minority within Canada as currently constituted. An independent Quebec would be up against exactly the same problem of cultural nationalism: how to integrate a community which lives its intimate life in a language other than that of the majority, and which will never assimilate. Think of it in Madison Grant's terms as "the indigestible mass of English Canadians" who would be present in an independent Quebec.

Reality differs from this simple analogy in one respect, and it is a difference which makes the situation even more difficult. It is simply that the French minority in Canada has never been the master of the English, while the English minority in Quebec obviously was for a long time the master of the French. That is, the English in Quebec have been marked by a history of mastery. No matter how hard they try, they simply don't know how to behave like a minority. Instead of speaking respectfully to the majority, their media heckle and harass and mock it. Polls show that the majority of Quebec anglophones, even now, think they know better than the French what is necessary for the survival of French culture in Quebec.[17]

It is this which creates a potentially tragic situation. The anglophones of Quebec, however attached they are to the French, will never willingly accept being ruled by them. It is reminiscent of the situation which arose when Czeckoslovakia gained independence from Germany, and the German-speaking minority marooned in the Czeck province of Bohemia refused to accept the authority of those they had formerly dominated.[18]

Emotionally— and the various philosophers of nationalism all agree that it is in the realm of emotion that the issue is ultimately decided— French Quebeckers belong to Quebec, and English Quebeckers belong to Canada. It is desperately sad that history has placed them on the same piece of earth.

There is no way to predict the outcome of the situation. It seems clear that many anglophones would leave an independent Quebec, but also that many would remain. What would happen to those who stay? Would an independent Quebec treat them the same way that Canada treated francophone minorities outside Quebec, by slowly and hypocritically strangling them? Would there be Quebec versions of Regulation 17? Would a French-speaking clone of Preston Manning (what a thought!) argue that it is all right for employers to shuffle their English employees to the back of the store so the customers aren't upset?

In short, would Quebec become an "ethnic" state?

There is still a good deal of confusion about this word "ethnic." Even the brief of the Quebec Teachers' Association, for all its lucidity, fails to explain exactly what it means by "the French-Canadian ethnic group."

Perhaps it would help to return to the Greek root of the word. *Ethnos* means nation, usually in the cultural rather than racial sense. "Ethnos" was the word that Isocrates used in the quote seen earlier in this book, saying that Greeks are those who share a culture rather than a kinship of blood.

In popular English usage, the meaning of the word has migrated somewhat. It usually describes a minority within a country. One would hardly call a resident of Paris an "ethnic Frenchman" in the same way that one can say a Quebecker is "ethnically French."

The word still has nothing to do with race. However, because it refers to minorities it takes on a coloration of the exotic which can become pejorative. The English-Canadian media, with that intellectual sloppiness which has always been its trademark, now uses the word "ethnic" almost interchangeably with "racial": as in, "Quebec threatens to become an ethnic state."

Because of this confusion, modern philosophers like Isaiah Berlin have re-examined the writings of philosophers like Herder and tried to decide what criteria to associate with the word "ethnic." Most serious writers on the subject today define it as having four attributes: shared language, territory, history and customs.

Nothing in this definition would prevent an ethnic Quebecker from having skin that is brown, black or yellow. It says nothing about physical traits. All four of the criteria which define ethnicity can be *chosen*.

When ethnicity is understood in this fashion, the familiar world around us suddenly takes on a very different appearance. It becomes clear, for example, that the United States of America is an "ethnic" nation. It tolerates no language but English.[19] The United States also imposes uniform school curricula which demand knowledge of its history. It has customs, such as the famous "sourire publicitaire" (publicity smile) whose insincerity baffles so many foreigners; not to mention a repertoire of vocal intonations, body slouches, and inexplicable pauses before answering a question which mark the speaker as American and nothing else.

The United States, like all the "first wave" modern nations owing allegiance to the civic ideals of the French revolution, does not see itself this way. It is officially committed to "civic" nationalism based on the freedom of the individual. But, as Noam Chomsky has so often demonstrated, the actual ambit of permitted opinions in the United States is narrow. There is wide public consensus on many subjects, and very limited tolerance of dissent.

It seems that the United States, along with France, has backed into "cultural" nationalism without officially admitting it. A game like baseball, supported by the American government in a conscious attempt to break down regional loyalties in favour of national ones, clearly belongs to the realm of collective or cultural nationalism.

In fact, the only modern democracy which has not clearly opted for cultural nationalism is Canada. We are still attempting to make a virtue of civic nationalism. Former culture minister Marcel Masse, who as a Quebecker was baffled by English Canada's indifference to cultural accomplishment, finally concluded that anglophone nationalism was oriented around nothing stronger than having the best medical insurance in the world. This, for lack of a better one, could serve as a thumbnail definition of civic nationalism.

To return, then, to Quebec.

Since Quebec is firmly committed to the model of cultural nationalism, an independent Quebec would almost certainly become an "ethnic" state in the sense just discussed. The policy of inter-culturalism already mandates that immigrants become familiar with Quebec's history and particular values. And, like every other major democracy, it would insist on the primacy of one language.

However, the 200-year history of the English language in Quebec would compel Quebec to recognize its status. Quebec would join those other small democracies, Belgium and Switzerland, in searching for an institutional framework to accommodate a small but unassimilable minority.

My intuition— and it can only be an intuition— is that Quebec, once released from the Procrustean bed of its current relationship with Canada, would demonstrate a surprising tolerance and even affection for its anglophone minority. Freed of the "visceral aversion of Quebec nationalism for Canada," francophones could finally acknowledge how much they have been influenced by centuries of cohabitation with the English, even down to their preference for bacon and eggs and hotel bars in small towns. Anglo-Quebeckers might well be granted the "recognition" which, in Christian Dufour's view, is currently denied them.[20]

This would leave English Canada alone with itself. That is not entirely a bad thing either. As political scientist Reg Whitaker has argued, it would be "an invitation to the rest of Canada to find its own authentic voice." The current doctrine of a national unity which includes Quebec means "that English Canada has no legitimate existence."[21]

This argument would seem to imply that I am in favour of the independence of Quebec. Certainly my colleagues have assumed this from the moment I expressed the least sympathy for the place.

But, surprisingly, I am not. I would like to see a "shell" federalism in which Quebec has most of the attributes of an autonomous country, and where the remaining nine provinces have a highly centralized government capable of managing the evolution of a meaningful cultural nationalism in English Canada. My belief in a strong central government betrays me as a Canadian cultural nationalist. My love for Quebec, however, leads me to believe that it requires a similar power to "centralize" its efforts within itself.

In a way, the question of Quebec independence— the question that lurks behind this book and torments the sleep of English Canadians— proves in the end to be almost beside the point. "English Canadians," writes Reg Whitaker, "should... get on with the task of defining themselves as a community, with or without Quebec."

Not only should, but must. The failure to do that will mark the true death of the dream of Canada— whether or not Quebec leaves it.

CONCLUSION

One of former British Prime Minister Margaret Thatcher's favourite aphorisms, it is alleged, is "There is no such thing as a community."

It is almost reassuring to see that a harsh philosophical idea can survive in pure form for over three centuries, and surface in the thinking of a powerful world leader of our time. Impervious to common sense, and the lived experience of billions of human beings, the cruel Calvinist apothegm goes marching on.

It is tempting to see the philosophical poles of individualism versus collectivism as the underpinnings of civic and cultural nationalism. But in practise, even the most rigorous defenders of individual-based doctrine seem to have acknowledged the existence of community. John Locke, who felt that "human society consists of a series of market relations,"[1] admitted nonetheless that the state could not simply allow the poor to starve in the streets. And John Stuart Mill, convinced as he was that the state exists to protect individual belief systems rather than to embody collective ones, accepted the legitimacy of ethnic states so long as there were populations which preferred them. For a group of individuals to choose to live as a political "ethnos" was in Mill's view a legitimate manner of pursuing happiness.

Since human beings create their personal identities dialogically, it is inevitable that we are influenced by the gestures, catch phrases and attitudes of those with whom we associate. The characteristics we associate with various national identities are one outcome of this process. Only Margaret Thatcher can know what sort of communities she feels do not exist, but can it possibly include the community of Englishmen?

It's a curious thing that, in spite of a centuries-old philosophical disposition against nationalism, England has evolved a national type which is one of the most recognizable and appealing in the world. It is perhaps also no coincidence that it has evolved one of the liveliest literary cultures on the planet. Aldous Huxley, only slightly tongue-in-cheek, wrote that it is largely "thanks to a long succession of admirable dramatists and novelists [that] Frenchmen and Englishmen know exactly how they ought to behave."[2]

That Huxley's example also includes France is a useful reminder that all the states which upheld the civic model of nationalism have long since— though usually without admitting it— evolved strong cultural identities and many of the characteristics of "ethnic" states. France in particular tended to define even a civic nationalism in collective rather than individual terms, a disposition which it passed on to Quebec.

English Canada, however, got caught neatly between the two conflicting models. In many respects it inherited the British Protestant model of extreme individualism, especially in the economic realm. But the challenge of settling a vast land mass with a tiny population seemed to call for a strong collective identity which could be imposed on immigrants, native Canadians and the French alike. For that purpose we borrowed Britain's cultural identity, and clung tenaciously to it for as long as possible.

But a borrowed cultural identity decays. As Arthur Lower noted in dismay at the end of World War II, no writers came forward to memorialize the nation's heroic achievement overseas, and politicians continued clacking their wooden jaws in the customary fashion. This, in his view, was not a sign of a diffident nation; it was a sign of no nation at all.

We then borrowed the American cultural model, and continue to make do with it. I have long been fascinated by novelist David Adams Richards' observation that Canadians, since they do not write songs celebrating their own cities, *think* of their own cities while singing "Kansas City" or "Abilene My Abilene."

It is not exactly a new observation that this is an unhealthy state of affairs. Fifty years ago E.K. Brown connected the poverty of Canada's literature to its "confused" state. "A great literature is the flowering of a great society, a vital and adequate society," he wrote. But he could not put his finger on the missing ingredient. "It is not in the province of a student of letters to say how a society becomes vital and adequate."[3]

Some tried to make a virtue of necessity, arguing that "the feeling of passivity and helplessness" was inevitable in a country caught on the fringes of British and American power. Since this state of affairs reflected the truth of our situation, perhaps "this very indistinctness," "apathy" and "face-lessness" was the beginning of a national identity.[4]

I can't imagine an identity inspired by facelessness.

A useful clue may lie in Charles Taylor's idea of dialogic identity. For a communal identity to evolve through the dialogues of individuals, it seems to me that the individuals in question must be able to take each other seriously— to *hear* each other— and that their conversation must contain a strong strain of optimism, a belief that the desired thing will come into existence.

In this sense, Canada's conversation with itself has often been interrupted: first by the ersatz "imperial" identity, then by the wishful American one, and finally by the Trudeau doctrine of national unity, which posited an impossible identity arising from the fusion of two communities which literally do not speak the same language.

It is interesting that all three of these disruptive episodes in our history are associated with hard-core liberal ideology, whose mistrust of human community is so well expressed by Margaret Thatcher.

The liberal idea of the sovereign individual was, in its historical origins, moral and admirable. Before this idea was articulated, human communities were almost universally oppressive and materially poor. Liberalism was an attempt to "liberate" the human talent and energy that was locked inside traditional polities which had become an obstacle to progress. It was this moral impulse, however misguided, which caused the early British settlers to detest the apparently medieval "community" they found in Quebec.

Even the Calvinist injunction to heap up wealth was, in its peculiar way, a moral doctrine, since it had to do with manifesting God's grace. The rich were enjoined to live austerely. The few surviving exponents of this view— at least one Canadian billionaire comes to mind— are rumoured to buy stale cookies and generally deprive themselves of the pleasures of their wealth.

Our problem is that for almost everybody else alive today, liberalism has lost its connection to austerity and self-discipline. Individualism has been hollowed out and come to mean little more than self-interest and material consumption. In his lecture series *The Malaise of Modernity*, Charles Taylor shows how in modern free-enterprise societies the choices made by individuals have become separated from value systems. The result is that we have a great deal of freedom— to make trivial and meaningless choices.

Traditionally, the power of imagination was connected to community. The conflicts which underlie literature and drama have to do with humans struggling to live together. The stern buccaneers of capitalism to whom Max Weber referred are unkindly treated in literature, which obeys a powerful internal impulse to show them harming their communities and ultimately destroying their own happiness.

Neither of the extremes of this great historic struggle is going to go away, because although antagonistic, both are necessary to create a successful modern nation. "The nationalists... were not altogether mistaken," writes A.D. Smith. "They grasped that if a nation, however modern, is to survive in this modern world, it must do so on two levels: the socio-political and the cultural-psychological."[5]

Canada has been very successful with the former, to which it owes its sterling reputation. But it has failed to develop a cultural-psychological dimension.

We are currently living in an era of right-wing triumphalism, because the socialist states which were advocated by some of Kant's successors have collapsed. Rhetorically, the Lockeian yawp of Margaret Thatcher, not to mention any number of neo-conservative journalists, is heard throughout the world. Behind this lies the undeniable truth that the free-enterprise system has succeeded materially to such an extent that most people can't imagine any other horizon of meaning for themselves than success, wealth and the *autonomy* which it supposedly brings. The idea of the individual is much more attractive today than the alternative.

And yet, apart from a few truly hard-core right wingers, most people know very well that we must live in community. There is a widespread nostalgia for a lost connectedness, and a growing suspicion that our lives are frenzied and acquisitive to no purpose.

But the voices which normally articulate community are in disarray. Culture, instead of being generated within communities, has become a commodity which can be produced and marketed. Indeed, although its solipsistic individualism cannot generate either values or stories, the free-enterprise system has become adept at mining the value systems of communities, commodifying them, and selling them back in the form of entertainments. The American historian Daniel Boorstin has called this the process of transforming a "people" into a "market."

Some version of this has been going on for at least a century, but it is only recently that intellectuals have developed doctrines to justify it. As a rule, they justify allowing the marketplace to invade every corner of human interchange by claiming that values shared by communities are false and manipulative. In this view, narratives are always oppressive, and artists who create them are the enemies of freedom. These doctrines set out to destroy the authority of anybody who speaks for their community in disinterested fashion, and to deny the existence of canons— that is, bodies of literature and art which incarnate the values of communities and nations.

This lofty dispute may seem remote from the lives of Canadians and Quebeckers. But we are subject, like people everywhere in the world today, to "the colonization of the individual through consumerization."[6]

The difference is that Quebec possesses a residual conservatism, expressed as cultural nationalism, which allows it to resist the new hegemony. Part of this impulse arises from Quebec's particular struggle to preserve its identity within Canada; part of it may come from the French tradition, which espoused "civic" ideals but tended to express them in collective form rather than following the extreme liberalism of Britain and the United States.

Whatever the blend of influences which created it, Quebec has been left with a functioning conservatism, in George Grant's sense of a society able to set goals for itself and to impose the discipline to achieve them. Quebeckers are comfortable with the phrase "projet de société." English Canadians, who have no idea how to go about a "project of society," find the expression unnerving.

One can't help but be struck in Quebec by the public conversation which, for example, takes Radio-Canada to task for being insufficiently intelligent in its programming, or condemns the least sign of electoral apathy. If you arrive late to renew a parking sticker, a clerk may gently reprove you for failing in your civic duty. Even drunkards howling in the street at two a.m. will listen to a passerby who confronts them, and try to defend themselves in complete sentences.

Business interests also genuflect before the general will. Shortly before the 1995 referendum Laurent Beaudoin, chairman of the mulitinational firm Bombardier, threatened to pull the company out of Quebec in the event of independence. His employees responded by plastering the plant with independence slogans, and demanded that Beaudoin withdraw the threat. He did so.

This kind of "conservatism," where even business must bow to the social consensus, is anathema to the triumphant liberalism of our day. I suspect that this, rather than the usual trumped-up charges of social or linguistic intolerance, is the real reason for the demential hostility of the Canadian financial press toward Quebec. Neo-conservatives do not support democracy as the average person understands it, but rather a narrow procedural democracy which does not regulate or otherwise touch upon market relations.

Six years ago American scholar Francis Fukuyama, in a now-famous essay called "The End of History," proposed that there could be no further challenges to liberal democracy.

Fukuyama's thoughts were inspired by the collapse of Marxism, but he made it clear that he believed all forms of communal social organization were finished, including nationalism. Like most right-wing intellectuals, he was part of "the neo-liberal dream of a world governed by commerce and free of strife."[7]

The right-wing euphoria was understandable, but short-lived. Nationalism in fact is a resurgent force in the world today. The reason is simple: "There is no evidence at all of public loyalties being transferred from national governments to supranational organizations."[8]

The problem for English Canada is that it has neglected the "cultural-psychological" side of nationalism. This makes it particularly difficult for English Canadians to acknowledge the nationalism of Quebec, whose strength in this respect tends to remind us of our own precariousness.

Much of Canadians' fragile self-esteem rests on the condition that Quebeckers must or should "love" us. Part of our progress toward political maturity must lie in accepting that they neither do nor should "love" Canada, and in admitting to ourselves that we do not— and cannot— "love" them. Patriotism, like individual human bonds, can only proceed from intimate knowledge. The experience of nations generally is that people cannot know each other across a language barrier. The intuitions of the nationalist philosophers about language seem to have been borne out by experience.

There are signs, nearly a year after the October referendum, that the large English-Canadian public is also coming to accept this difficult truth. In my view this is a benediction: it means we can finally get on with the job of building the English-Canadian nation.

This does not necessarily mean that Quebec will go the full route to independence. The presence of the United States has always been a good reason for English and French Canadians to seek mutual support, and remains so. But the Québécois, for reasons that this book has hopefully made clear, have never felt a sense of belonging to the entity called "Canada"; and it is unlikely they ever will. The only useful relationship between the two peoples would seem to be a contractual one, based on mutual need and benefit.

If English Canada can accept this, it will follow logically that we must provide ourselves with those aspects of nationhood which are emotional. We must transform "the rest of Canada" into a beloved place.

This task has been made more difficult by the political marginalizing of Canadian nationalists during the past decade. Since the failure of Diefenbaker and Trudeau to assert Canada's interests against those of the United States, the political mainstream has moved away from nationalism. The only surviving national party, the Liberals, is on its knees to the United States and to the international business community alike. Those who are trying to roll the stone back up the hill today often do so with the meagrest of political resources.

But within the Canadian community, nationalism is still a central concern. Even writers suspicious of it, such as Michael Ignatieff, are forced to admit that no-one has conceived a viable alternative to the nation state. There are even popular writers such as Richard Gwyn who now argue that Canada must protect the values established by the early English settlers who "set down the tramlines" on which Canada, however unsteadily, still runs today.[9] This is an extraordinarily conservative sentiment in a liberal era where we imagine that we can re-kit our nation every season as if it were strutting on a fashion runway. It approaches the basic truth that a nation is a certain kind of thing, and there are ground rules for creating it which are not subject to tinkering.

The modest contribution of this book has been to demonstrate that one of these ground rules is cultural unity. That is, that it is necessary to undertake our project of *cultural* nationhood without Quebec. The myth of a "national unity" encompassing two linguistic groups has caused us to waste precious decades.

For English Canada to define itself as a "people" implies no disrespect for Quebec. We will better appreciate Quebec when we have come to appreciate ourselves.

It is no coincidence that the harshest feelings toward Quebec are demonstrated by those who preach the doctrine of a two-culture "national unity" so fervently. As I write this conclusion, *Saturday Night* magazine has just published another brutal, ignorant diatribe against Quebec, remaining true to a century-long tradition. At the same time, newspapers are arguing for a massive airlift of assistance to victims of the July flood in the Saguenay region— as a means of proving our "love" for that most separatist of regions.

This is a dismal and confused situation. But it is also an old situation, an old reaction, part of the now-exhausted dynamic of the English-French struggle in Canada. Thoughtful Canadians, I believe, are ready to move on.

The next step lies in the word "recognition," as it has been discussed in this essay. It is true that English Canada has not "oppressed" French Canada in the overt fashion that other countries have oppressed linguistic minorities. But we have demonstrated a similar hardness; there is harshness in our literature, and a willed forgetting of our history. We have failed in the task of recognition.

It is important to recognize this failure, but not in order to flagellate ourselves. Rather, we should see in it our humanity, and our human limits. To admit this to ourselves is the beginning of wisdom.

From there, if we are fortunate, we will find a way to accept that only the minority knows what it requires as a condition of self-respect and "épanouissement." We may design the first federal state in the world in which a minority can be said to have been "recognized" as an equal partner.

We must also accept that such a solution may not be possible. The

French are declining as a percentage of Canada's population, and they may conclude that there is no possible federal arrangement which can ensure their long-term survival. There is much political theory to back them on this point. Liberal governments, as Jurgen Habermas has pointed out, are not in the business of protecting collective rights. They cannot ensure the *future* survival of minority languages.

If we cannot invent a new kind of liberal government, then we should in all good grace let Quebec leave.

In any event, the real issue is that English Canada must become a cultural nation. This challenge cannot be avoided, whether Quebec stays or leaves.

Northrop Frye once observed that it is "conventional for Canadian criticism to end on a bright major chord of optimism about the immediate future."[10]

Perhaps we can agree that the time for bright chords of optimism has passed. The process by which a people gives itself a cultural identity is a mysterious one, and there is no way of knowing whether English Canada will succeed.

But by acknowledging the task that lies before us, we can at least know that we have set out in the right direction.

ACKNOWLEDGEMENT

This book could not have been written without the prior work of the many English Canadians who have tried in all good will to think their way to a solution of the Canada–Quebec problem. Foremost among them is philosopher Charles Taylor, whose ideas have influenced much of what is valid in this essay, but which are not responsible for its shortcomings.

I am also grateful to the many English-Canadian writers, critics and historians who have devoted their lives to the affectionate study of French Canada. Their work has been indispensable to me.

There are authors cited here, such as Fernand Dumont, who are important to Quebec's evolving internal dialogue, but who have not been translated. There are also indispensable reference works, such as *Le Choc de langues*, which are unlikely ever to appear in English. I hope that the reader will find as much pleasure in reading the quotations from these works as I did in translating them.

NOTES

INTRODUCTION

1. Canadian Dualism, xviii
2. Two Solitudes, 362
3. Journal, 38
4. Ibid, 70
5. History of Canada, preface

CHAPTER ONE

1. Journal, 71
2. Murther and Walking Spirits, 302: quoted in Le Devoir, 9 December 1995
3. Blood and Belonging, 6
4. Nationalism, Alter, 10
5. Sources of Self, 415
6. Lament for a Nation, 21
7. Stand To Your Work, 51
8. Sources of Self, 167
9. Stand To Your Work, 52
10. The Unknown Dominion, 58
11. Ibid, 38
12. Nationalism in Canada, 20
13. Canada, Quebec, and the Uses of Nationalism, 16
14. Lament, 65
15. Ibid, 68
16. Ibid, 68
17. Ibid, 33
18. Ibid, 76
19. Two Solitudes, 159
20. The Globe and Mail, 1 February 1995
21. Nationalism, Kedourie, 115
22. Blood and Belonging, 24

CHAPTER TWO

1. Isaiah Berlin, New York Review of Books, 21 November 1991, 19
2. Nationalism, Kedourie, 37-8
3. Immanuel Kant, 53
4. Isaiah Berlin, New York Review of Books, 21 November 1991, 19
5. The Protestant Ethic, 112
6. Ibid, 106
7. Ibid, 72
8. Sources of Self, 101
9. After the Nation-State, 8
10. Empire of the St. Lawrence, 40
11. Ibid, 157
12. Canada, Quebec, and the Uses of Nationalism, 190
13. Nationalism, Kedourie, 57
14. Malaise of Modernity, 29
15. Nationalism, Kedourie, 37
16. A note on terminology: In North America, "liberal" often refers to left-of-centre political beliefs, while "conservative" is associated with the right and especially the American notion of rugged individualism. For this reason, hard-line right wingers are called neo-conservatives in current parlance. Historically, however, the terms had opposite meanings. A liberal was a defender of individualism, while a conservative tended to uphold the community's traditional values, and indeed, the idea of community itself. The terms are often used this way still in England and Europe, where a hard-line right winger may be referred to as a "neo-liberal." In this book, the European usage is generally but not always followed. As a rule, context will make the meaning plain.
17. After the Nation-State, 15
18. This is sometimes called "trade nationalism," and it is worth

noting that the Canadian Manufacturers' Association supported this approach until 1984, when it finally yielded to American and global pressure and came out in favour of the Free Trade Agreement. Source: True Patriot Love, 24

19. True Patriot Love, 28

20. Abbé Groulx: Variations on a Nationalist Theme, 16

21. Isaiah Berlin, New York Review of Books, 21 November 1991, 20

22. The Creators, 226

23. Nationalism, Kedourie, 73

24. Nationalism, Kedourie, 71

25. Une Histoire du Québec, 16

26. Nationalism in Canada, 47

27. Une Histoire du Québec, 16

28. L'Identité fragmentée, 301

29. Le Québec à la minute de vérité, 106

30. Ray Conlogue, The Globe and Mail, 25 January 1995

31. Ramsay Cook, The Globe and Mail, 28 January 1995, D5

32. Nationalism in Canada, 62; 64

33. Canadian Dualism, 9

34. Colony to Nation, 66

35. telephone conversation, 25 April 1996

36. Du Canada au Québec, 275

37. Ibid, 278

38. Les Têtes à Papineau, 24

39. Les Québécois, 16

40. Le Choc des langues: Francis Masères, 1766 letter to British government, 100

41. Les Québécois, 35

42. France in America, 58

43. Introduction to Canadian Fiction, 119

44. Les Québécois, 112

45. Colony to Nation, 45

46. After the Nation-State, 5

47. Ibid, 5

48. France in America, 112

49. Du Canada au Québec, 202

50. Colony to Nation, 43

51. Du Canada au Québec, 188

52. Ibid, 199

53. A Source-Book of Canadian History, 40

54. France in America, 133

55. A Source-Book of Canadian History, 40

56. Genèse, 84

57. France in America, 112

58. Ibid, 276

CHAPTER THREE

1. Le Défi québécois, 114

2. The Dream of Nation, 76

3. Colony to Nation, 248

4. The Durham Report, 294-295

5. Ibid, 40-41

6. from Hansard, 1891, McCarthy speech: Le Choc des langues, 258

7. Notre Société et son roman, 48

8. from L'histoire du Canada: Du Canada au Québec, 286

9. La terre paternelle, 108

10. The Ethnic Origins of Nations, 191

11. Jean Rivard, introduction

12. Colony to Nation, 216

13. Genèse, 156

14. Ibid, 148

15. Ibid, 170

16. Le Choc, 125

17. French-Canadian and Quebec Novels, 54

18. The Dream of Nation, 48

19. Ibid, 55

20. Genèse, 173

21. Ibid, 173

22. Ibid, 138

23. Introduction to Canadian Fiction, 256

24. The Dream of Nation, 53

25. Ibid, 53

26. Genèse, 222

27. Le Choc, 148

28. Genèse, 249

29. Crémazie, 27

30. Ibid, 27

31. Introduction to Canadian Fiction, 133

32. Les anciens canadiens, 106

33. Ibid, 33

34. Ibid, 152

35. Ibid, 213

36. Charles Guérin, 29

37. The Sash Canada Wore, 142-143

38. Genèse, 247

39. Studies on Canadian Literature, 166

40. Ibid, 165

41. Notre société et son roman, 54; 33

42. Canadian Dualism, 9

43. Donald C. Macdonald, reviewing a biography of Howard Ferguson, Globe and Mail, 24 September 1977: quoted in The Sash Canada Wore, 154

44. Menaud, 11

45. Ibid, 48

46. Ibid, 79; 117

CHAPTER FOUR

1. Marie Calumet, 77

2. Crémazie, 67

3. Le murmure marchand, 110

4. Le Courage et lucidité, 37

5. Nationalism in Canada, 241

6. Ibid, 238

7. Ibid, 5

8. The Bush Garden, 134

9. Identity and Community, 48

10. The Imperialist, 124

11. Ibid, 44

12. Ibid, 202

13. Ibid, 74

14. Notre Milieu, Montreal, 1942: quoted in Colony to Nation, 70

15. La Maison suspendue, 14

16. Identity and Community, 47

17. Masks of Fiction, 46

18. Racial Attitudes in English-Canadian Fiction, 6

19. Ibid, 58

20. Ibid, 7

21. Passing, 72-3: quoted in Racial Attitudes in English-Canadian Fiction, 4

22. Ibid, 42

23. Ibid, 42

24. Second Image, 23

25. Debts to Pay, 43

26. Le Défi québécois, 67

27. Debts to Pay, 41

28. Le Défi québécois, 66

29. Canada, Quebec, and the Uses of Nationalism, 178

30. Ibid, 180

31. Le Choc, 247

32. Ibid, 256

33. Montreal Mon Amour, xix

34. Two Solitudes, 1

35. Introducing Hugh MacLennan's Two Solitudes, 18

36. Ibid, 32

37. Ibid, 25

38. Montreal Mon Amour, 212

39. Home Truths, 224

40. Ibid, 236

41. English Canada Speaks Out, 18

42. Nationalism in Canada, 249

43. Masks, 18

44. Nationalism in Canada, 235

45. The Bush Garden, 133

46. Le murmure marchand, 31

47. What Is a Canadian Literature?, 35

48. Making It Real, 57; 61; 63

CHAPTER FIVE

1. Beautiful Losers, 125-129

2. Intolerance, 132

3. The Rocking Chair, 16

4. Juifs et réalités juives, 212

5. Introducing The Apprenticeship of Duddy Kravitz, 46-7

6. The Street, 56

7. Identity and Community, 51

8. Ibid, 111

9. Juifs et réalités juives, 263

10. Ibid, 265

11. Ibid, 275

12. Oh Canada! Oh Quebec!, 156

13. Ibid, 89

14. Ben-Z. Shek, "Mordecai Richler: Further Debate," Outlook, September 1992, 22

15. On the Jews of Lower Canada, 228

16. Ben-Z. Shek, "Mordecai Richler: Further Debate," Outlook, September 1992, 10

17. Footnote: In fact, as researcher Pierre Anctil has pointed out in L'Actualité (December 1991, 22), exactly 12 anti-Jewish editorials appeared in Le Devoir during the 1930's "during a precise historical period." Such editorials disappeared after 1939, and from the 1950's the newspaper has been overtly positive toward the Jewish community. "Richler's phrase is therefore unjust and unacceptable."

18. Earth and High Heaven, 74

19. Juifs et réalités juives, 297

20. The Traitor and the Jew, 204

21. Ibid, 207

22. Anglophobie, 442

23. Ibid, 445

24. Oh Canada! Oh Quebec!, 243

25. Le Syndrome des plaines d'Abraham, 107

26. Racial Attitudes, 126

27. Identity and Community, 122-3

CHAPTER SIX

1. quoted in Le Devoir, 5 January 1996

2. paraphrased in 1888 by Arthur Buies: Le Choc des langues, 232

3. Reconciling, 101

4. Le Choc, 196

5. L'Actualité, 15 November 1994, letters page

6. Spare Parts, 49

7. Immersion experts Merrill Swain and Sharon Lapkin, quoted in the Globe and Mail, 7 October 1989, D2, article by Orland French

8. Globe and Mail, 23 November 1991, D3, article by Deborah Jones

9. Colony to Nation, introduction to 1977 edition

10. "Reading Between the Poles: The 'English' French-Canadian Canon," 12

11. Ibid, 15

12. Ibid, 23

13. Le Défi québécois, 155

14. Canadian Modern Languages Review, May 1987, 702

15. Canadian Modern Languages Review, April 1995, article by J. Claude Romney

16. Second Image, 132-33

17. Reconciling, 46

18. Ibid, 46

19. Ibid, 47

20. Imagining Ourselves: Classics of Canadian Non-Fiction, 325

21. Les actes retrouvés, 199-200

22. Reconciling, 167

23. Les actes retrouvés, 192

24. Reconciling, 48

25. Ibid, 51-53

26. Le Choc, 81

27. Colony to Nation, 462; 559

28. En pièces détachées, 19; 66

29. Boundaries of Identity, 87

30. Ibid, 86-87

31. Le Choc, 123

32. Ibid, 140

33. Ibid, 164

34. History of Canada, Volume 2, 214

35. Le Choc, 82

36. quoted in Nationalism, Kedourie, 62

37. Les actes retrouvés, 193

38. Le Choc, 132

39. En pièces détachées, 76-77

42. The Dragonfly of Chicoutimi, 61

43. Ibid, 21

44. Ibid, 24

CHAPTER SEVEN

1. Le murmure marchande, 81

2. Sept Jours, L'événement de lundi, etc.

3. quoted in Making It Real, 37

4. quoted in Globe and Mail, 7 October 1995, C1

5. quoted in Globe and Mail, 1 December 1995, A21

6. from interview notes for an article published in the Globe and Mail, 27 August 1990, N10

7. Malaise of Modernity, 40

8. Multiculturalism, 130

9. Gregory Baum, "Ethnic Pluralism in Quebec," Canadian Forum, April 1996, 20

10. brief to the Bélanger-Campeau Commission, excerpted in Boundaries of Identity, 175

11. Montreal Gazette, 2 August 1996, B3

12. quoted in Journal, 149-151

13. Globe and Mail, 4 November 1995, D4

14. La Guerre, Yes Sir!, 99-101

15. The Poetical Works of William Henry Drummond, 222

16. Ibid, xxii

17. A 1991 CROP poll, for example, showed that 89 per cent of Quebec anglophones are still opposed to Bill 101 even though they know that the French consider it absolutely essential to their linguistic survival.

18. Nationalism, Kedourie, 115

19. A Quebec friend of mine discovered this when she and her boyfriend were posted to Washington, D.C. Chatting to each other in French one day, they were approached by a youth who asked what language they were speaking. Flattered, they told him. "Well, stop doing it," he replied. "It bugs me."

20. Le Défi québécois, 93-94

21. English Canada Speaks Out, 19

CONCLUSION

1. The Political Theory of Possessive Individualism, 263

2. Nationalism in Canada, 242

3. What Is a Canadian Literature?, 102

4. Frank Watt, quoted in Nationalism in Canada, 247

5. After the Nation-State, 242

6. Ibid, 222

7. Ibid, 200

8. Nationalism and National Integration, 224

9. Nationalism Without Walls, 113

10. The Bush Garden, ix

BIBLIOGRAPHY

Abbé Groulx: Variations on a Nationalist Theme, Susan Mann Trofimenkoff. Copp Clark, Vancouver, 1973

Les actes retrouvés: essais, Fernand Ouellette. Les Éditions HMH, Montreal, 1970

After the Nation-State, Mathew Horsman and Andrew Marshall. Harper Collins, London, 1995

Anglophobie: Made in Quebec, William Johnson. Stanké, Quebec, 1991

Around the Mountain, Hugh Hood. Peter Martin Associates, Toronto, 1976

Beautiful Losers, Leonard Cohen. McClelland and Stewart, 1991

Blood and Belonging, Michael Ignatieff. Penguin Books, Toronto, 1993

Boundaries of Identity, ed. William Dodge. Lester Publishing, Toronto, 1992

The Bush Garden, Northrop Frye. House of Anansi Press, Toronto, 1971

Du Canada au Québec, Heinz Weinmann. L'Hexagone, Montreal, 1987

Canadian Dualism, eds. Mason Wade and Jean-C. Falardeau. University of Toronto Press, 1960

Canada, Quebec, and the Uses of Nationalism, Ramsay Cook. McClelland and Stewart, 1986

Canadians of Old (Les anciens canadiens), Philippe Aubert de Gaspé, trans. Georgiana M. Pennée. G.&G. Desbarats, Quebec, 1864

Charles Guérin, Pierre-Joseph-Olivier Chauveau. Re-issued by Guérin, Montreal, 1973

Le Choc des langues au Québec 1760-1970, Guy Bouthillier and Jean Meynaud. Les Presses de l'Université du Québec, 1972

Colony to Nation, Arthur Lower. Longmans Canada, Toronto, 1946

Le Courage et la lucidité, Jacques Dufresne. Les Éditions du Septentrion, Sillery (Quebec City), 1990

The Creators, Daniel Boorstin. Random House, New York, 1992

Crémazie, Michel Dassonville. Fidès, Montreal, 1956

Debts to Pay, John F. Conway. James Lorimer and Company, Toronto, 1992

Le Défi québécois, Christian Dufour. l'Hexagone, Montreal, 1989

The Dragonfly of Chicoutimi, Larry Tremblay. Les Herbes rouges, Montreal, 1995

The Dream of Nation, by Susan Mann Trofimenkoff. Gage Publishing Limited, Toronto, 1983

The Durham Report. Oxford Clarendon Press, London, 1912

Earth and High Heaven, Gwethalyn Graham. Jonathan Cape, Toronto, 1944

Empire of the St. Lawrence, Donald Creighton. Macmillan, Toronto, 1956

English Canada Speaks Out, eds. J.L. Granastein amd Kenneth McNaught. Doubleday Canada, Toronto, 1991

The Ethnic Origins of Nations, Anthony D. Smith. Basil Blackwell, London, 1986

"Ethnic Pluralism in Quebec," Gregory Baum. Canadian Forum, April 1996

The Forgotten Quebeckers, Ronald Rudin. Institut québécois de recherche sur la culture, Quebec City, 1995

France in America, W.J. Eccles. Fitzhenry and Whiteside, Canada, 1972

La Genèse de la société québécoise, Fermand Dumont. Boréal, Montreal, 1993

La Guerre, Yes Sir!, Roch Carrier. Stanké, Montreal, 1991

The Poetical Works of William Henry Drummond, William Henry Drummond. G.P. Putnam's Sons, New York, 1912

Une Histoire du Québec: vision d'un Prophète, Maurice Séguin. Guérin, Montreal, 1995

History of Canada, François-Xavier Garneau, trans. Andrew Bell. Richard Worthington Publishers, Montreal, 1866

Home Truths, Mavis Gallant. Macmillan of Canada, Toronto, 1981

L'Identité fragmentée, Gilles Bourque and Jules Duchastel. Fidès, Montreal, 1996

Identity and Community, Irving Massey. Wayne State University Press, Detroit, 1994

Imagining Ourselves: Classics of Canadian Non-Fiction, ed. Daniel Francis. Arsenal Pulp Press, Vancouver, 1994

Immanuel Kant, by Lucien Goldmann, NLB Press, London, 1971

The Imperialist, Sara Jeannette Duncan. McClelland and Stewart, Toronto, 1971

Intolerance, Lise Noel. McGill-Queen's University Press, Kingston/Montreal, 1994

Introducing Hugh Maclennon's Two Solitudes, Linda Leith. ECW Press, Toronto, 1990

Introducing Mordecai Richler's The Apprenticeship of Duddy Kravitz, George Woodcock. ECW Press, Toronto, 1990

George Woodcock's Introduction to Canadian Fiction, George Woodcock. ECW Press, Toronto, 1993

Jean Rivard, Antoine Gérin-Lajoie. McClelland and Stewart, 1977

Le Journal (tenu pendant la commission royale d'enquête sur le bilinguisme et le biculturalisme), André Laurendreau. VLB Éditeur, Montreal, 1990

Juifs et réalités juives, Pierre Anctil and Gary Caldwell. Institut québécois de recherche sur la culture, Quebec, 1984

Lament for a Nation, George Grant. McClelland and Stewart, 1965

Lord Durham, Chester W. New. Oxford Clarendon Press, 1929

La Maison suspendue, Michel Tremblay. Leméac, Montreal, 1990

Making It Real, Robert Lecker. House of Anansi Press, Toronto, 1995

The Malaise of Modernity, Charles Taylor. House of Anansi Press, Concord, Ontario, 1991

Marie Calumet, Rodolphe Girard, trans. Irène Currie. Harvest House, Montreal, 1976

Masks of Fiction, ed. A.J.M. Smith. New Canadian Library, 1961

Menaud, Maître-Draveur, Félix-Antoine Savard. La Corporation des Éditions Fidès, 1992

"Montreal," A.M. Klein. (In Complete Poems, Volume 2, 261.) University of Toronto Press, Toronto, 1990

Montreal Mon Amour, Selected and Introduced by Michael Benazon. Deneau, Toronto, 1989

"Mordecai Richler: Further Debate," Ben-Z. Shek. Outlook, September, 1992

Le murmure marchand, Jacques Godbout. Boréal, Montreal, 1984

Mythe et image du Juif au Québec, Victor Teboul. Éditions de Lagrave, Montreal, 1977

Multiculturalism and the Politics of Recognition, Charles Taylor. Princeton University Press, 1992

Murther and Walking Spirits, Robertson Davies. McClelland and Stewart, 1977

National and Ethnic Movements, eds. Jacques Dofny and Akinsola Akiwowo. Sage Publications Inc., 1980

Nationalism, Elie Kedourie. Hutchison of London, 1960

Nationalism, Peter Alter. Edward Arnold, London, 1989 (division of Hodder Headline group)

Nationalism and National Integration, Anthony Birch. Irwin Hyman, London, 1989

Nationalism in Canada, University League for Social Reform, ed. Peter Russell. McGraw-Hill, Toronto, 1966

Nationalism Without Walls, Richard Gwyn. McClelland and Stewart, 1995

Notre société et son roman, Jean-Charles Falardeau. Éditions HMH, Montreal, 1967

Oh Canada! Oh Quebec!, Mordecai Richler. Viking, New York, 1992

On the Jews of Lower Canada and 1837-38, Volume 3, David Rome. National Archives of the Canadian Jewish Congress, 1983

En pièces détachées, Michel Tremblay. Leméac, Montreal, 1972

The Political Theory of Possessive Individualism: Hobbes to Locke, C.B. Macpherson. Clarendon Press, Oxford, 1962

The Protestant Ethic and the Spirit of Capitalism, Max Weber. Charles Scribner's Sons, New York, 1958

Le Québec à la minute de vérité, Michel Brunet. Guérin, Montreal, 1995

Les Québécois, Marcel Rioux. Éditions du Seuil, Montreal, 1974

Racial Attitudes in English-Canadian Fiction 1905-80, Terrence Craig. Wilfrid Laurier University Press, Waterloo, 1987

Reading Between the Poles: The "English" French-Canadian Canon, Cynthia Sugars. Unpublished graduate paper, 1996

Reconciling the Solitudes, Charles Taylor. McGill-Queen's University Press, Kingston/Montreal, 1993

The Rocking Chair, A.M. Klein. Ryerson Press, Toronto, 1948

The Sash Canada Wore, Cecil Houston and William Smyth. University of Toronto Press, 1980

A Season in the Life of Emmanuel, Marie-Claire Blais. McClelland and Stewart, 1992

Secessionist Movements in Comparative Perspective. Pinter Publishers, London, 1990

Second Image, Ronald Sutherland. New Press, Toronto, 1971

A Source-Book of Canadian History, J.H. Stewart Reid. Longmans Canada, Toronto, 1959

Sources of the Self, Charles Taylor. Harvard University Press, Cambridge, Mass., 1989

Spare Parts, Gail Scott. Coach House Press, Toronto, 1981

Stand To Your Work: A Summons to Canadians Everywhere, W. Eric Harris. The Musson Book Company, Toronto, 1927

The Street, Mordecai Richler, Weidenfeld and Nicholson, London, 1972

Studies on Canadian Literature, ed. Arnold E. Davidson. Modern Languages Association of America, New York, 1990

Le Syndrome des plaines d'Abraham, Eric Schwimmer. Boréal, Montreal, 1995

La terre paternelle, Patrice Lacombe. Hurtubise HMH, 1972

Les Têtes à Papineau, Jacques Godbout. Éditions du Seuil, 1981

The Traitor and the Jew, Esther Delisle. Robert Davies Publishing, Montreal, 1995

True Patriot Love, Sylvia B. Bashevkin. Oxford University Press, 1991

Two Solitudes, Hugh MacLennan. Macmillan of Canada, Toronto, 1945

The Unknown Dominion, Bruce Hutchison. Herbert Jenkins, London, 1942

What Is a Canadian Literature?, John Metcalf. Red Kite Press, Guelph, 1988